THE MAXIMILIANEUM IN MUNICH

THE MAXIMILIANEUM IN MUNICH

Scholarship Foundation · Building · Bavarian Parliament

Text
Lothar Altmann

Translation
Margaret Marks

Photographs
Wolf-Christian von der Mülbe

Verlag Schnell & Steiner · Regensburg

Vorsatz/Nachsatz: *The Maximilianeum after its completion. View c. 1880*

Schutzumschlag: *The show front of the Maximilianeum from the northwest – view of Munich from the Stone Hall*

Die Deutsche Bibliothek – CIP-Einheitsaufnahme

The Maximilianeum in Munich : scholarship foundation, building, Bavarian parliament / text Lothar Altmann. Transl. Margaret Marks. Photogr. Wolf-Christian v. d. Mülbe. – Regensburg : Schnell und Steiner, 1993
  Dt. Ausg. u. d. T.: Das Maximilianeum in München
  ISBN 3-7954-1053-3
NE: Altmann, Lothar; Mülbe, Wolf-Christian von der, Marks, Margaret [Übers.]

1st edition 1993

© Verlag Schnell & Steiner GmbH, Regensburg
All rights reserved
Reproductions: Grafisches Systemhaus bt gravure gmbh, Neutraubling
Printer: Erhardi Druck GmbH, Regensburg
Printed in Germany
ISBN 3-7954-1053-3

Contents

The Scholarship Foundation 7
    The Founder 7
    The History of the Scholarship Foundation 9
    The "Historical Gallery" 12

The Building 30
    The Architectural and Planning History 30
    The Architect 50
    The Exterior and its Sculptures 52
    The Interior and its Furnishings 66

The Bavarian Parliament 127
    History of the Bavarian Parliament 127
    The Bavarian Landtag 132
    The Bavarian Senate 142

Literature 144

Sources of Illustrations 144

The Scholarship Foundation

The Founder

King Maximilian II of Bavaria (1811–1864) was only 21 years old and still Crown Prince of the Kingdom of Bavaria when he formed the plan to erect "a large national building on the Isar heights at Munich" to "enhance the people's national and monarchist sentiments". To this plan he soon added the idea of an "Athenaeum", an institution whose aim was "to support talented Bavarian youths [of every class] in attaining that degree of academic and intellectual attainment required for the solution of the more exalted tasks of service to the state"; it was modelled on similar institutions in France and England and in other German-speaking cities (Tübingen, Berlin, Dresden and Vienna). Max II studied history, philosophy and political economy at the universities of Göttingen and Berlin and furthered his general education on journeys to London, Paris, Rome, Constantinople and Athens, and he would have liked to be a professor himself. After his accession to the throne in 1858 he encouraged academic study and education in Bavaria; for example, he appointed outstanding scholars from the whole of Germany above all to posts at the University of Munich, he founded the Maximilian Order for Science and Art, he sponsored the first German industrial exhibition at the Munich Crystal Palace, he founded the Germanisches Nationalmuseum in Nuremberg, the Bayerisches Nationalmuseum in Munich and the Historical Commission at the Bavarian Academy of Sciences, and he was also involved in school reform. He spared no efforts "to open all doors to intellectual enquiry, so that Bavaria should not lag behind the developments of the age". Under the rule of Max II, ministerial accountability, free elections, the separation of the executive and the judiciary, jury courts, freedom of the press and freedom of assembly were introduced in Bavaria, the manorial system of land ownership was repealed and a system of welfare for workers was begun – all measures intended to serve the "alleviation of the material and spiritual oppression of the Bavarian people".

◁ *King Max II of Bavaria. In the background the building of the Maximilianeum, painting in the study foundation*

Commemorative plaque in the study foundation

The History of the Foundation

In 1852, the "Athenaeum" – in 1857 it was finally given its present name of *Royal Maximilianeum* after its founder – was provisionally established in a rented building in Amalienstrasse near the University. The scholarship holders were six young men who had completed their Abitur (schoolleaving examination), chosen from the then 28 grammar schools of Bavaria and the Palatinate; these pupils were enabled to study law and political science at the university without material worries. According to the statute, they were to be pupils who had "distinguished themselves from others of their age in both intellectual and moral respects". The theologian Anton Hannecker was appointed the first chairman of the foundation (1852–1866). From 1858 on, students of the faculties of philosophy and natural science were also supported, but these two groups were each to constitute only one-sixth of the total number of scholarship holders.

Max II, who created the foundation and gave it his name, unfortunately did not live to see the completion of the institute building, and it was only under his son and successor King Ludwig II that the foundation was given its legal form: by the deed of 1876, the foundation owned the Maximilianeum building and also a gallery of paintings of historical scenes and marble busts, and this is still the case today; at that date the capital of the foundation was 800,000 guldens. According to the final "Basic Provisions for the Royal Maximilianeum", the institution could now admit 26 "youths of outstanding intellectual ability and irreproachable moral conduct". They were required to be "in possession of Bavarian citizenship and of the Christian faith". Students of theology and medicine were not admitted. Even today, the scholarship holders still receive free board and lodging.

After the end of the monarchy in 1918, the sponsorship of the Maximilianeum, in accordance with the will of its founder, passed to the Ludwig Maximilian University of Munich (although for the time being it was exercised by the government); this has remained the case up to the present day. The severe inflation of the 1920s in Germany rapidly consumed the foundation's capital, so that the only meagre source of income that remained was the entrance fees of the gallery. As a result, the foundation was now dependent on contributions from the Ministry of Education and Cultural Affairs; the scholarship holders themselves also had to make a contribution. The financial situation did not improve until, in 1949, the Bavarian Parliament, which had been bombed out, moved into the Maximilianeum in return for an annual rent of 70,000 DM and an undertaking to be responsible for the maintenance of the building.

Since 1980, the "Wittelsbach Jubilee Foundation" has granted scholarships to the 26 youths and also to 10 gifted young women from Bavaria, although at

Library of the study foundation

present the latter cannot live in the Maximilianeum for lack of space. Thus, since the institution was created, approximately 800 students of both sexes have enjoyed the advantages of the foundation. Some famous recipients of Maximilianeum scholarships have been the Minister of Economics of the German Reich Eduard Hamm (1879–1944; in office 1923–1925), the two Bavarian Chief Ministers Eugen Ritter von Knilling (1865–1927; in office 1922–1924) and Franz Josef Strauß (1915–1988; in office 1978–1988) and the physicist Werner Heisenberg (1901–1976).

◁ *Lounge and study in the study foundation*

The "Historical Gallery"

Wilhelm Doenniges was the first person commissioned by Max II with the planning of the "Historical Gallery". In 1850 Doenniges wrote: "A series of pictures ('oil paintings') is to be executed, with the purpose of illustrating the most important moments of world history through art. – The task is both to educate the people and to develop art itself in a deliberately prescribed direction (historical painting) which has received too little favour in the past. – History is not only the Last Judgement, but also the educator of humanity". In his "Instruction for Artists" he also wrote: "The conception and execution of historical pictures should be that of a serious, strict and elevated style. – Although beauty must be the principal rule, art should never depart from truth. Therefore it is necessary to avoid all elements of genre, petty subjects, even prettiness and mannerism, and the whole costume ... of the epoch must be recorded. The artists are obliged to adhere strictly to their task, that is, to present the idea of history truthfully. For this reason the moment which is to be represented is given to them in the form of a historical sketch."
Eventually, under the direction of Leo von Klenze (from 1852), 30 oil paintings were executed and exhibited in the three rooms on the first floor of the west wing of the Maximilianeum. 17 of these survived the Second World War; they are now distributed in various rooms and corridors of the Bavarian Parliament and the scholarship foundation, since the south and north rooms have been used as plenary assembly halls by the Bavarian Landtag and the Bavarian Senate since 1949. One of the historical paintings is on display in the Neue Pinakothek, on loan from the foundation. In addition, several oil sketches have been preserved in the Bayerisches Nationalmuseum and in the Bavarian State Painting Collections.
According to the "List of paintings ... of the Royal Maximilianeum" of 1884, the historical paintings were classified in three historical periods: "Antiquity", "The Middle Ages" and "The Modern Period", and arranged in the following chronological sequence: "Centre hall. Left: 1. The Fall, by Alexander Cabanel (Paris) ... – South hall. 3. Building of the Pyramids (c. 1500 B.C.), by Prof. Gustav Richter (Berlin) ... 4. Belshazzar's Feast in Susa (538 B.C.), by Karl Otto ... 5. The Naval Battle of Salamis (480 B.C.), by Wilhelm von Kaulbach (Munich). 6. The Age of Pericles, by Philipp Foltz (Munich). 7. The Olympic Games, by Georg Hiltensperger (Munich). 8. The Wedding of Alexander the Great and the Daughter of Darius in Susa (324 B.C.), by Andreas Müller (Munich). 9. The Capture of Carthage by Scipio Africanus (146 B.C.), by Georg Conräder (Munich) ... 10. The Birth of Christ, by Johann Schaudolph (Munich). 11. The Battle of Arminius in the Teutoburg Forest (9 A.D.), by Friedrich Gunkel (Rome). 12. The Heyday of Rome under Emperor Augustus, by Georg Hiltensperger. 13. The Crucifixion of Christ, by Wilhelm Hauschild

Julius Köckert: Harun al Raschid receives Charlemagne's envoys (786), painting in the study foundation

(Munich). 14. The Resurrection of Christ, by Ernst Deger (Düsseldorf)." "Centre hall ... Right: 2. Mohammed's Entry into Mecca. Destruction of the Kaaba (627), by Andreas Müller (Munich)." Of all these oil paintings, only "The Naval Battle of Salamis" survived the Second World War; it can now be seen in the Plenary Assembly Hall of the Bavarian Landtag.

"Northern hall. 15. Harun al Raschid receives Charlemagne's Envoys (786) ... by Julius Köckert (Munich). 16. The Coronation of Charlemagne (800), by the court painter Friedrich Kaulbach (Hanover) [today on the south wall of the Stone Hall]. 17. The Battle of Hungary near Augsburg (955), by Michael Echter (Munich) ... 18. Emperor Henry IV in Canossa (1077), by Eduard Schwoiser (Munich) ... 19. The Capture of Jerusalem by Gottfried von Bouillon (1099), by Karl von Piloty ... 20. Emperor Frederick Barbarossa and Duke Henry the Lion in Chiavenna (1176), by Philipp Foltz (Munich) [today beside the "Naval Battle of Salamis" in the Plenary Assembly of the Landtag]. 21. Emperor Frederick II and his Court in Palermo (1230), by Artur von

Banquet held on 4th September 1928 on the occasion of the laying of the foundation stone for a research building for the Deutsches Museum in the south gallery room (illus. left) and the north gallery room (illus. right), now the plenary assembly halls of the Landtag and the Senate

Ramberg ... [now on loan to the Neue Pinakothek]. 22. Imperial Coronation of Ludwig the Bavarian in Rome (1328), by A. Kreling (Nürnberg) [today on the north wall of the Stone Hall]. 23. Luther at the Diet of Worms (1521), by Julius Schnorr von Carolsfeld (Dresden). 24. Queen Elizabeth I of England inspecting her army in sight of the Spanish Armada (1588), by Ferdinand Piloty. 25. Founding of the Catholic League by Duke Max I of Bavaria (1609), by Karl von Piloty. 26. Peter the Great founds Petersburg (1703), by the Russian court painter Alexander Kotzebue (Munich). 27. Battle of Zorndorf (1758), by Albrecht Adam (Munich). 28. Louis XIV ... receiving a Genoese Legation at Versailles ... (1686), by Ferdinand Pauwels (Weimar). 29. Washington Forces the British General Cornwallis to surrender Yorktown (1781), by Eugen Hess (Munich). 30. Battle [of the Nations] at Leipzig (1813), by Peter Hess (Munich)".

The "Historical Gallery" was supplemented by the pictorial programme of other rooms of the Maximilianeum and by the façade. According to the above-mentioned list, there were also 24 busts of Carrara marble by the Munich sculptors Peter Schöpf and Johann Halbig placed along the two colonnades of the "piano nobile", representing benefactors, inventors, sages, men of literature, statesmen and military commanders.

The idea of a "Historical gallery" was put into practice several times in Germany in the 3rd quarter of the 19th century. At an earlier date than the Maximilianeum in Munich, the staircase of the Neues Museum in Berlin was given a cycle of colossal paintings of scenes from the history of humanity, commissioned by King Frederick William IV of Prussia, and the Altes Bayerisches Nationalmuseum (today the Völkerkundemuseum – Museum of Ethnology) in Munich, at the request of King Max II of Bavaria, received a series of scenes from Bavarian history modelled on the historical sequence of paintings "à toutes les gloires de la France" in the residence at Versailles.

At first it was intended that the best German and also foreign historical painters should be obtained for the "Historical Gallery" of the Maximilianeum, which was created in 1850–1874. But for financial reasons it was eventually necessary to restrict the artists largely to the teachers and students of the Munich Academy of Visual Arts. Thus the painting collection of the Maximilianeum in Munich at the time of its creation was not only "important for the study of history", but also a "gallery of historical paintings by the most outstanding [Munich] masters of the time", which displayed the development of 19th-century historical painting in Munich from classicism through Biedermeier to the Gründerzeit, the period of rapid industrial expansion in Germany from 1871–1873, and in doing so showed clearly the transformation of this genre of painting under King Max II.

Michael Echter: The Battle of Hungary on the Lechfeld (955), painting in the festive hall of the study foundation

Karl Theodor von Piloty: The Capture of Jerusalem by Gottfried von Bouillon (1099), painting in the study foundation

Eduard Schwoiser: Emperor Henry IV in Canossa (1077), painting in the study foundation

Philipp Foltz: *The Humiliation of Emperor Frederick Barbarossa by Henry the Lion (1176)*, painting in the Plenary Assembly Hall of the Bavarian Landtag

Julius Schnorr von Carolsfeld: Luther at the Diet of Worms (1521), painting above the entrance to the dining room of the study foundation

Ferdinand Piloty: Queen Elizabeth I of England inspects her army in sight of the Spanish Armada (1588), painting in the study foundation

Karl Theodor von Piloty: Foundation of the Catholic League by Maximilian I of Bavaria (1609), painting in the dining room of the study foundation

23

Albrecht Adam: Battle of Zorndorf (1758), painting in the festive hall of the study foundation

◁ *Alexander von Kotzebue: Peter the Great founds St. Petersburg (1703), painting in the study foundation*

Ferdinand Pauwels: Louis XIV receives a Genuese delegation at Versailles (1686), painting in the study foundation

Eugen Hess: Surrender of the Fortress of Yorktown to Washington (1781), painting in the study foundation

Peter von Hess: Battle of the Nations at Leipzig (1813), painting in the study foundation

The Building

The Architectural and Planning History

In his 1839 list of projects which were to be realized after his accession to the throne, Crown Prince Maximilian included a "connection between the city and the Isar from the New Residence over the Lehel district". This project assumed a more concrete form when, on 4th March 1851, the architect Friedrich Bürklein presented King Max II with plans "relating to the embellishment of Munich": in these plans, this connection between the old town of Munich and the borough of Haidhausen, which was incorporated into Munich in 1854, was defined for the first time as a sequence of a street, the "forum", bridges and an "acropolis". The royal motto was "I will have peace with my people", and in the spirit of this motto the aim of the project was to create a boulevard and a centre of urban communication. In contrast to Ludwigstrasse, above all private buildings with rented flats, shops, cafés, restaurants, theatre halls etc. were to be erected, culminating in "an acropolis – an elevated object, a picturesque point, directly connected to the city and interacting with it". Thus it would be possible to open up the Lehel district with its narrow winding streets and to cultivate the marshy terrain endangered by floods. In 1853, work began on building the "Neue Strasse", approximately 1200 m in length, which from 1858 on was officially named *Maximilianstrasse*; in the process of building the so-called forum, designed in the form of a Roman circus, the plan developed further and further away from the originally intended park to a street planted with grass and trees modelled on the Champs-Elysées in Paris, which was finally closed at the north by the building of the government of Upper Bavaria (by Friedrich Bürklein 1856–1864) and at the south by the Bayerisches Nationalmuseum (today the National Museum of Ethnology, by Eduard Riedel 1858–1865). The bronze statues (1856–1868) of four important figures of the early 19th century were here presented as models to the citizens of Munich: the Bavarian General Count Deroy (by Johann von Halbig), the American physicist, philanthropist and statesman Count Rumford (by Kaspar Zumbusch), the philosopher Friedrich Wilhelm von Schelling (by Friedrich Brugger) and the optician Joseph von Fraunhofer (by Johann von Halbig); in place of the originally planned memorial column in the circular flowerbed of the forum, the monument to King Max II (design by Kaspar Zumbusch) – with personifications of the virtues of a ruler and genii of the four Bavarian tribes (Bavarians, Swabians, Franconians and Palatinates) on the pedestal – was erected here in 1875. On the occasion of the 700th anniversary of the

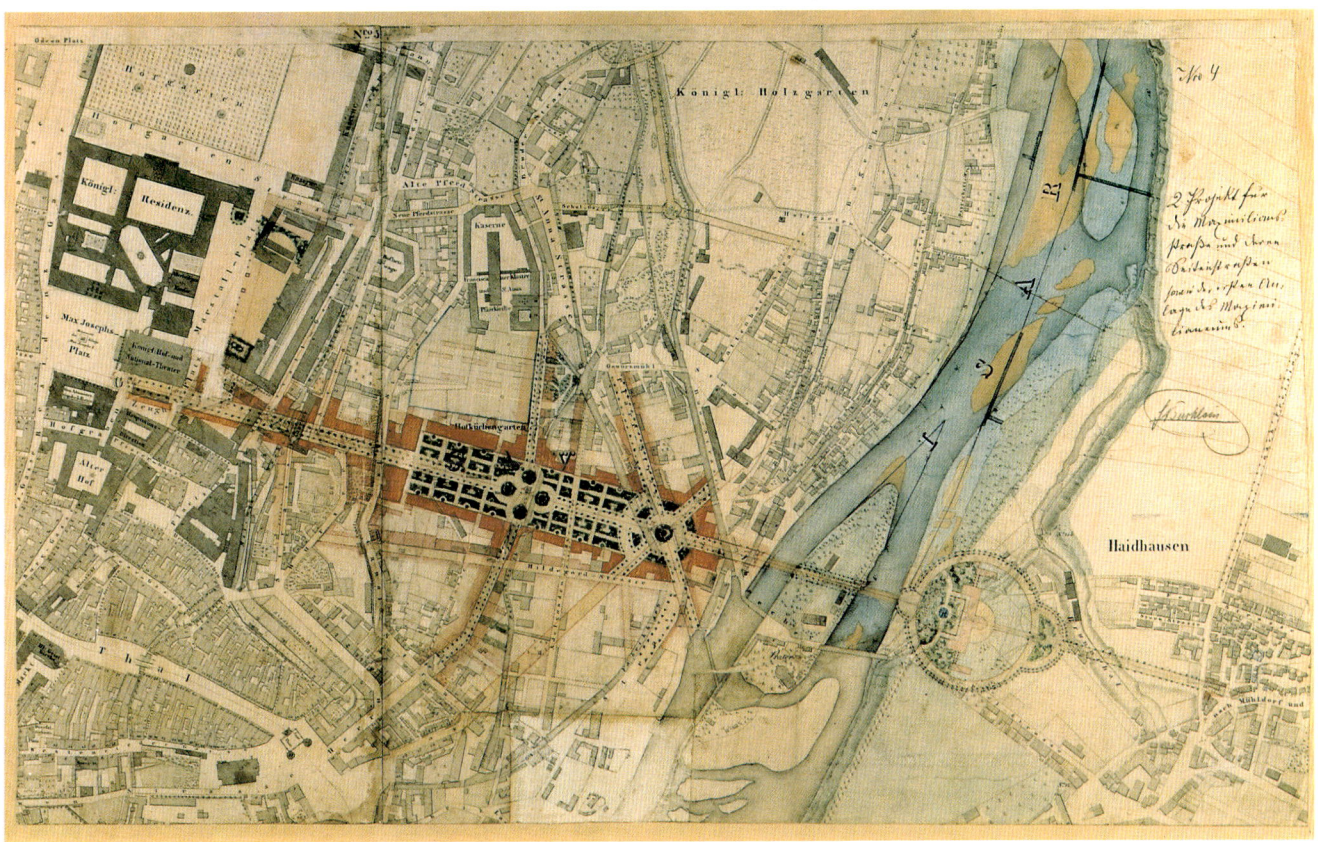
Friedrich Bürklein: Second project for Maximilianstraße in 1852, reproduktion in the Bürklein room of the Landtag restaurant

foundation of the city in 1858, the municipal building officer Arnold Zenetti built the two bridges across the Isar and the Prater island (at the beginning of the 20th century these bridges were replaced by the present wider bridges by Friedrich von Thiersch); when they were opened on the King's name day in 1863, the first vehicle to cross them was a street locomotive by Maffei, symbolizing the age of technology.

In order to give Munich's new show street a uniform appaearance, Max II commissioned the architects Friedrich Bürklein, Rudolf Wilhelm Gottgetreu, Eduard Riedel, August Voit and George Friedrich Ziebland as early as 1852 to design model façades. These were to observe a new style prescribed by the King, the so-called *Maximilian style:* on the basis of a neo-Gothic style influenced by Anglo-Saxon models, the best from all historical stylistic epochs

Building site of the Maximilianeum c. 1857, photograph in the Munich city archives

Building of the Maximilianeum (c. 1865)

was to be combined with modern technology. Characteristic of this style are the use of a skeleton construction technique using cast iron, the predominance of vertical lines (emphasized by so-called "elongated lesenes"), the pointed-arch arcading as a leitmotif, the cladding of façades with terracotta, the light, cheerful, almost graphical overall impression and the way in which the show front and the interior of the building are divided into storeys at different levels.

The planning of the *Maximilianeum* proceeded parallel to that of Maximilianstrasse. In 1845 Eduard Metzger (1807–894), a pupil of Gärtner and Professor at the Munich Polytechnikum, produced first designs for it, in keeping with the requirements of an institution of education which had been laid down by the philologist Friedrich von Thiersch; these designs, however, were rejected, not least because of their use of the round arch. After the present site had finally been chosen, Max II commissioned the architect Ludwig Lange (1808–1868) with the planning; but the project which he presented in 1848 was also rejected because it did not correspond to the King's expectations.

For this reason, Max II decided in 1850 to issue an "invitation to a competition relating to the preparation of a construction plan for an institution of higher education and teaching", published in German, English and French, one of the biggest international architectural competitions of the 19th century. The text of the invitation to compete was a manifesto of the Maximilian style, for example in the following: it is hoped to "create an edifice whose total appearance will unmistakably and quite clearly express the character of the age ... Today's architecture has ... all the achievements of the past at its disposal by way of models and techniques. A skilful architect will use the available architectural forms ... with their ornamentation in complete freedom to satisfy the present age, and will combine them to create an original, beautiful, organic whole". One qualification was emphasized: that this was a case of "the creation of a building in Germany in the German spirit and interests, so that it might appear appropriate when creating the design not completely to overlook ... the formal principles of old German, so-called Gothic architecture and when designing the ornamentation ... [not to overlook] ... the use of German animal and plant forms". Finally the desire was expressed that "the sister arts of painting and sculpture in their broadest sense should also be employed, in order to create a superb monument of art and education characteristic of the present age and significant in all its elements".

In view of these conditions it is not surprising that the envisaged closing date for entries (31st July 1851) had to be extended twice for lack of applicants, and that the jury had to decide on only 17 entries. In 1854, the first prize was in fact awarded to the Wilhelm Stier (1799–1856), a Berlin senior government building officer and pupil of Schinkel, but Max II rejected his "imaginative" design, not only for reasons of cost. He now without further ado entrusted the project to Friedrich Bürklein, whose plan for the embellishment of the city had shown how well he could adapt to the King's ideas and wishes, and who did not disappoint the King on this occasion either.

After the plot of land had been acquired, a process which was not without friction, Max II laid the foundation stone of Bürklein's building on 6th October 1847, a day of storm and rain, in the presence of all his ministers of state, the President of the government, the Rector of the University and the governing bodies of the Academy of Sciences, the Maximilianeum and the Pagerie. The necessary earth-moving work (levelling down and filling in) and the erection of the massive substructures was a long-drawn-out process. Meanwhile, Karl Effner laid out the Maximilian gardens north of the area. On 28th November 1861 the last beam was positioned in the top storey of the east end,

*Friedrich Bürklein:
Design for the
Maximilianeum,
reproduction in the
Bürklein room
of the Landtag
restaurant*

Friedrich Bürklein: Plan of façades of the Maximilianeum with pointed arches, reproduction in the Bürklein room of the Landtag restaurant

reserved for the scholarship foundation (and occupied from 1863 at the latest). On 5th February 1864, shortly before his unexpected death, the King announced a decisive change in his plans, although the central section of the west end had already been raised to above first-floor level. This change was the result of growing criticism of the project, and it constituted a capitulation of the Maximilian style; the intended pointed-arch arcades, which can be seen in Bürklein's design in the Munich Stadtmuseum and in the painting by Engelbert Seibertz in the present-day conference room, were replaced by "un-German" neo-Renaissance arches, and the lesenes were replaced by an order of columns (pilasters). Thus the architectural and planning history of the Maximilianeum marks the beginning and the end of the Maximilian style. After the death of the King, who had paid the building costs from his private purse, the project could be financed to a large extent only from the interest on the foundation's capital, and as a result the completion of the work was delayed: only in 1872 was the last of the scaffolding removed from the show front; in 1874 the building was finally complete inside and outside – the style

Rebuilding after destruction in the Second World War

was simpler than had been intended, and in parts the work was badly executed, as was soon to appear. Only twenty years later the large brick surrounding wall had to be completely rebuilt; in 1902 the weathered frescoes in the tympanums were replaced by mosaics by the Royal Bavarian Court Institute of Mosaic Art Rauecker and Solerti in Munich; in 1933–35 the terracotta facing of the west façade had to be renewed.

Until 1918, the Maximilianeum housed not only the scholarship foundation and a "historical gallery" but also the royal "Pagerie" (school for pages). The efforts of the National Socialists to establish a party headquarters here were thwarted. Until shortly before the end of the war, the Munich Art Exhibition was held in the rooms of the gallery, and in the arcades the "highest café in Munich" invited guests to enjoy a "magnificent panoramic view of the city and of the distant mountains". But the Second World War made its presence felt in the Maximilianeum as elsewhere when anti-aircraft units, parts of the Land Statistics Office and the Academy of Music were quartered there. Two-thirds of the building were destroyed by bombing.

The conference room after its destruction in the war

It was therefore a stroke of good fortune that the Bavarian Landtag chose the Maximilianeum as its seat, although its members wanted to oust the scholarship foundation when the Landtag first moved in. After both parties had come to an agreement, the Landtag became a tenant on 11th January 1949, making certain alterations necessary in what had previously been the rooms of the gallery. The building soon became too small, and in 1958/59 and 1964/65 wings containing offices, parliamentary chambers and a small swimming pool were added at the east end. When this in turn was no longer big enough, in 1979, a semi-circular extension along the east surrounding wall was planned, which would have made it necessary to demolish the two new wings. However, the decision to carry out this 70-million-DM project was never finally taken, so that two buildings in the immediate neighbourhood were acquired as an alternative. Since 1978, a thorough renovation of the Maximilianeum has been under way, in the course of which frescoes and stuccowork which had been painted over have been revealed again, bricked-up arches have been reopened and (as already happened in 1962/63) the terracotta facing of the west façade has been renewed; at the same time the Landtag restaurant was redesigned: on the walls of its garden room, paintings by Eckard Hauser now present a charming view of the Bavarian Alpine foothills. At present the decorative paintings in the arcades are gradually being restored. In 1990, Prof. Gerd Winner of the Academy of Visual Arts in Munich created a series of 24 paintings in mixed techniques: views of the Maximilianeum. In 1993 an underground car park was built beneath the Maximilianeum. In autumn 1994 the building work to extend this car park on the east side (design by Volker Staab, Berlin), retaining the postwar section, wll be completed.

View of Munich from the Stone Hall ▷

41

Anteroom to assembly rooms I and II

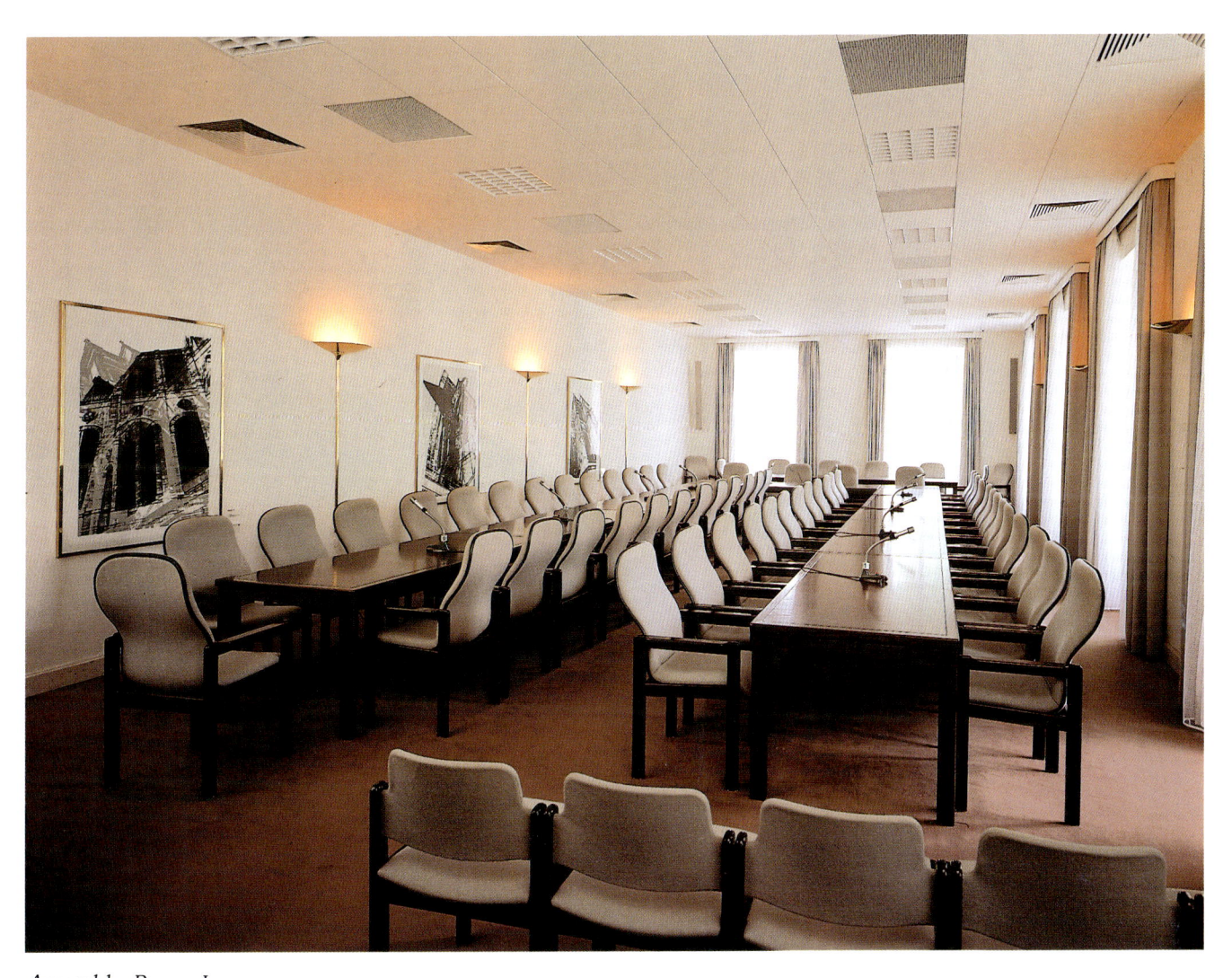

Assembly Room I

Assembly room in the Landtag members' house Max-Planck-Straße 5

Elmar Göppl: Place and Being, granite sculpture consisting of several pieces in the inner courtyard of the Landtag members' house Max-Planck-Straße 5

Gerd Winner: Maximilianeum Nike, painting in mixed techniques in the corridor outside the President's office

Gerd Winner: Maximilianeum XXIV, painting in mixed techniques in assembly room V in the Landtag

The Architect

Friedrich Bürklein was born on 20th March 1813 in Burk near Ansbach, the son of a teacher. From 1828 on – like his younger brother Eduard eight years later – he studied under Friedrich von Gärtner at the Academy of Visual Arts in Munich; he was to become the most successful and famous pupil of this professor of architecture after Gottfried Semper. In 1836 he passed the qualifying examination for the civil service. In 1840/41 he was permitted to accompany Gärtner to supervise the building of the Residence of King Otto in Athens. Bürklein was first active as an architect of private houses (above all in the university district) and of villas in and around Munich; in these buildings he remained indebted to the style of his teacher. In 1843 he took the post of a building director at the Railway Building Commission in Nuremberg; two years later he was transferred to the General Administration of the royal railways in Munich, and in 1846, on behalf of the government, he visited tall railway structures in Germany, Austria, Belgium, Holland, France and England. It was partly as a result of this that numerous Bavarian state railway stations were erected after Bürklein's plans, for example those in Ansbach, Augsburg, Bamberg, Hof, Nördlingen und Rosenheim. His most spectacular railway station building, however, was that of Munich in 1847–1849, in the round arch style; its boldly constructed main hall attracted the attention among others of King Max II, who in 1850 appointed Bürklein professor at the Polytechnische Schule in Munich and promoted him to government building officer (later senior government building officer and officer of the executive board) at the executive board of the royal transport offices. In 1853 the King took Bürklein with him on his journey to Rome. Without doubt, Bürklein's main work is the layout of the Maximilianstrasse in Munich, together with the buildings there of the government of Upper Bavaria (1856–1864), the former Mint (1857–1863) and the Maximilianeum. His "Frauengebäranstalt" (women's childbirth institution, 1853–1856) in Sonnenstrasse, today the Postal Savings Office, represents an important step from the late Gothic of the Wittelsbach Palais (now destroyed) in the direction of the Maximilian style. Bürklein was a broken man after the failure of this style realized by him, the death of his patron Max II and the loss of his eldest son, who fell at Sedan, and he died on 4th December 1872 in the Werneck sanatorium in Lower Franconia. His son Gottfried became well-known as a painter of seascapes and landscapes.

Franz Moos: The architect Friedrich Bürklein, lithography ▷

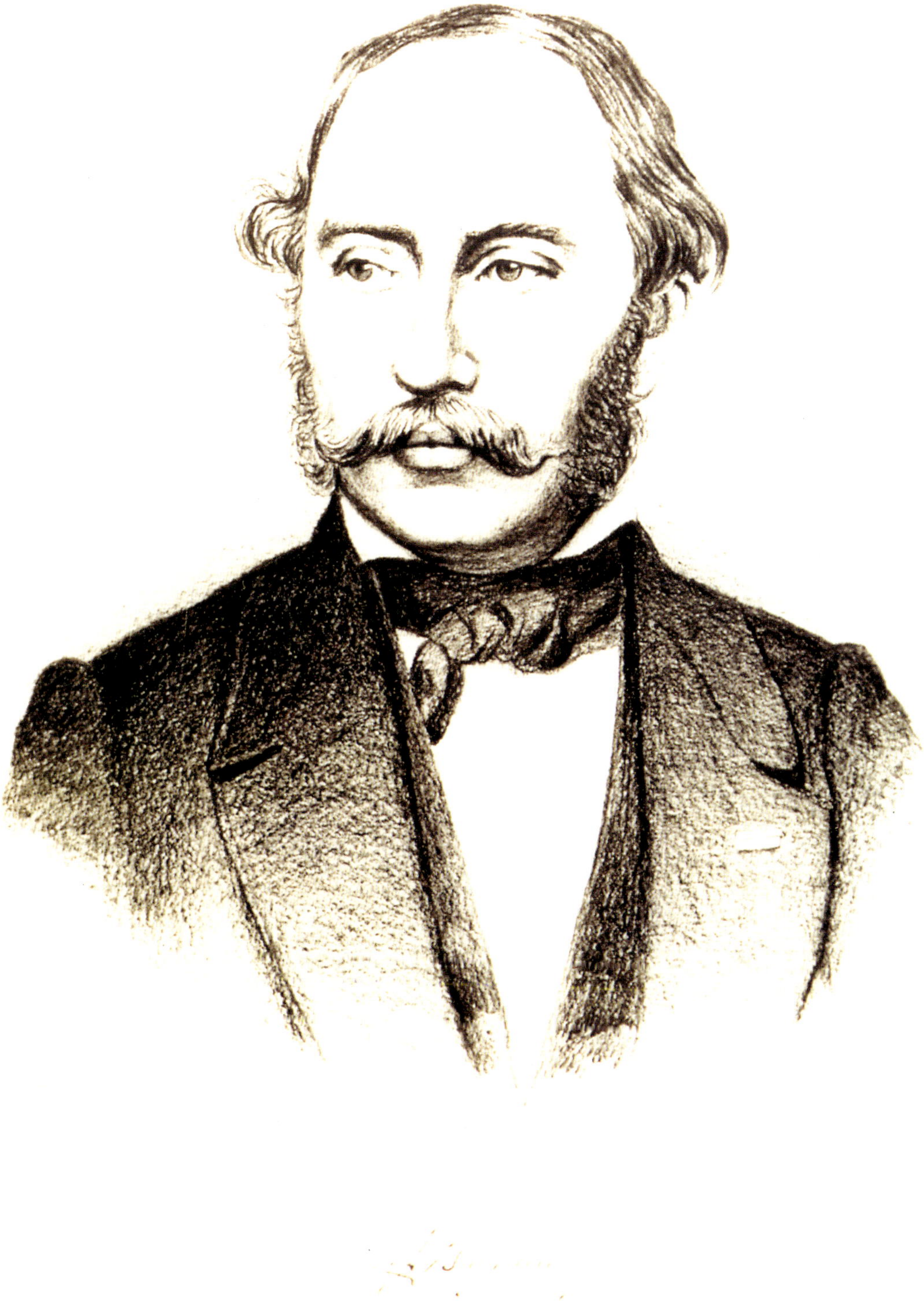

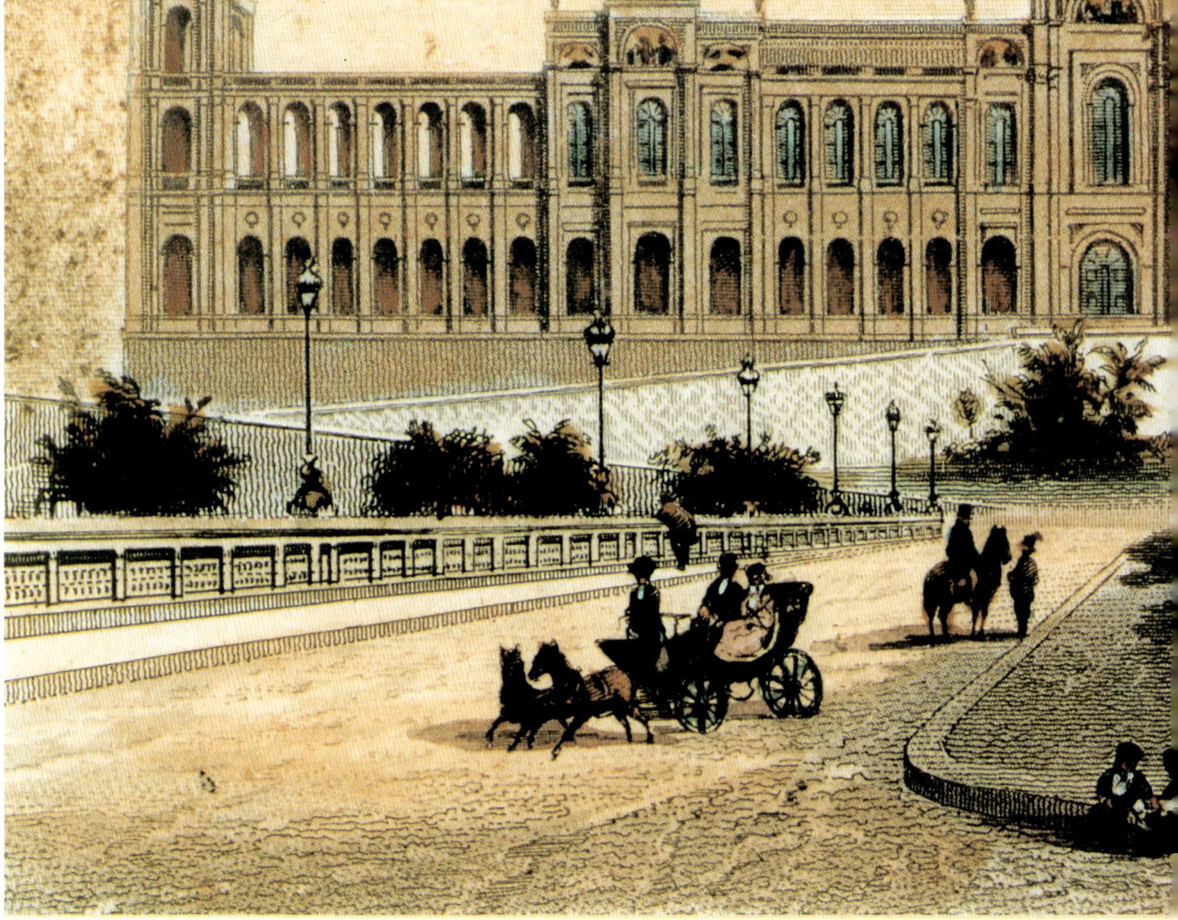

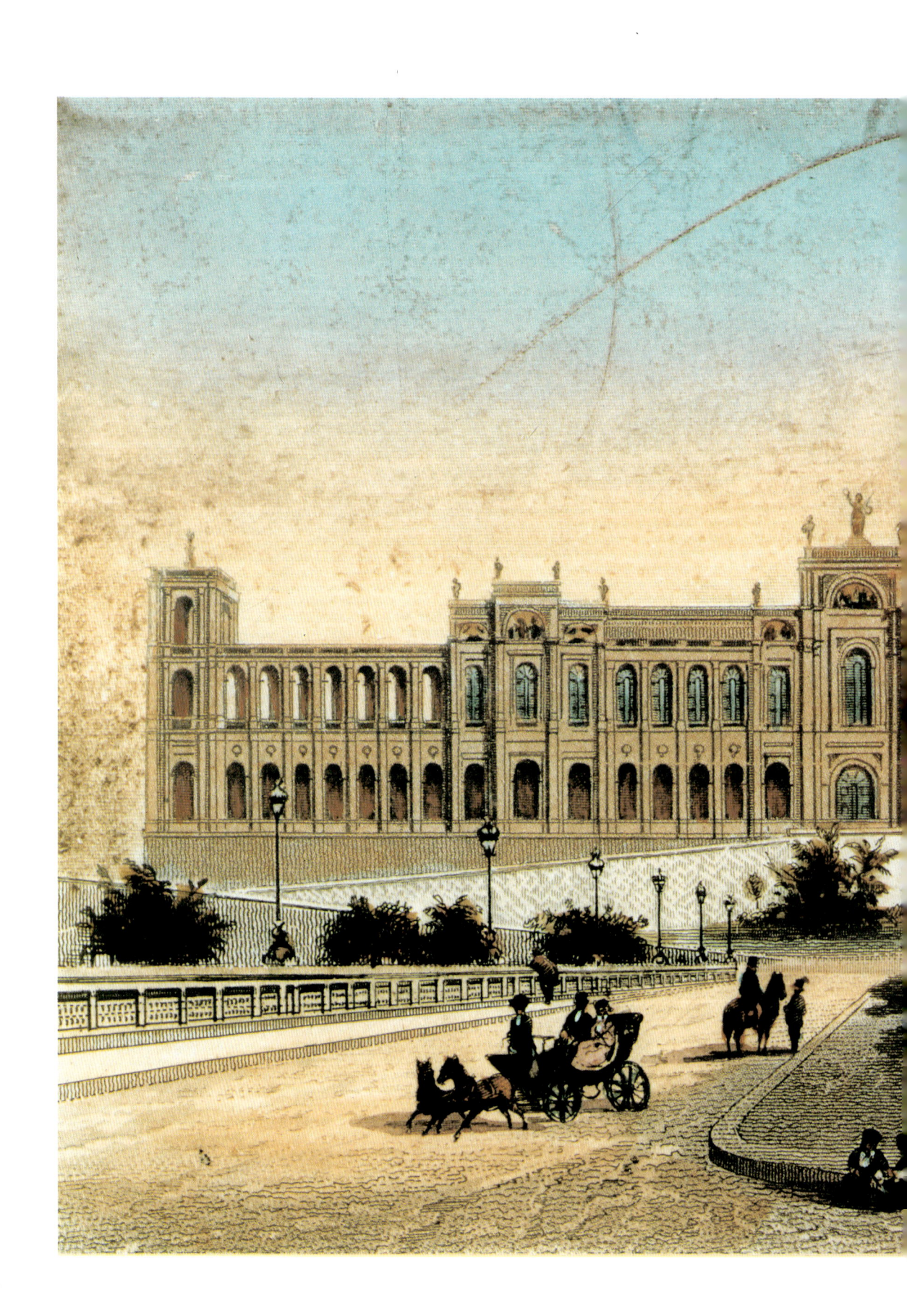

View of the Maximilianeum 1864, drawing in the Bürklein room of the Landtag restaurant

The Exterior and its Statues

The extensive building dominates the east bank of the Isar, its broad driveway opening it effectively to public view. It rises like a backdrop, similar to a gloriette as a point de vue of the Maximilianstrasse. Its splendour is enhanced when the terracotta facing and the mosaics in the gable area shine in the light of the evening sun. The *show front* with its flat roof, resting on a high pedestal, is composed of a slightly concave centre section and two straight side wings. The regular rows of round arches in both storeys are closed at each end by a three-storey tower, and the three projections in the centre section divide them into two rows of seven outer and two rows of four inner axes in a rhythmic pattern. The lower row of arcades is open to the west for its whole length; the upper is open at both ends in the wings but glassed in at the centre, which reduces the heaviness of the building. In the centre the three-axis central projection rises like a pavilion above the show front, emphasized in its central axis by higher arches and culminating in the figure of Nike, the Goddess of Victory (cast pewter by Max Widmann (?)). The two side projections of the central section are similarly structured; these too, in the piano nobile, are characterized by the Corinthian order of columns in place of the pilaster arrangement and are overtowered by an attic with pictures in semi-circular tympanums. In this way the most important interior rooms of the building are marked on the exterior; the so-called Stone Hall in the centre, the present conference room in the north, and the present reading room in the south.

The *statues on the west façade* can be seen from a distance and proclaim the programme of the original "institution of higher education and teaching". Thus, for example, the mosaics on the centre projection, which were created in 1902 and modelled on the original frescoes, show the endowment of the courtly Benedictine monastery of Ettal by Emperor Ludwig IV the Bavarian in 1330 as an example of the piety and charity of the Bavarian ruling dynasty, flanked by the foundation of the University of Ingolstadt by Duke Ludwig IX the Rich in 1472 and the victory of the Franconian poet Wolfram von Eschenbach in the singers' competition at the Wartburg as an example of science and art, which had flourished in "Bavaria" from time immemorial. These pictures, whose theme was prescribed by Max II, and of which oil sketches have been preserved in the Maximilianeum, are based on works by Karl Theodor von Piloty (1826–1886), a professor at the Munich Academy and painter of historical scenes.

Centre projection of the show front ▷

53

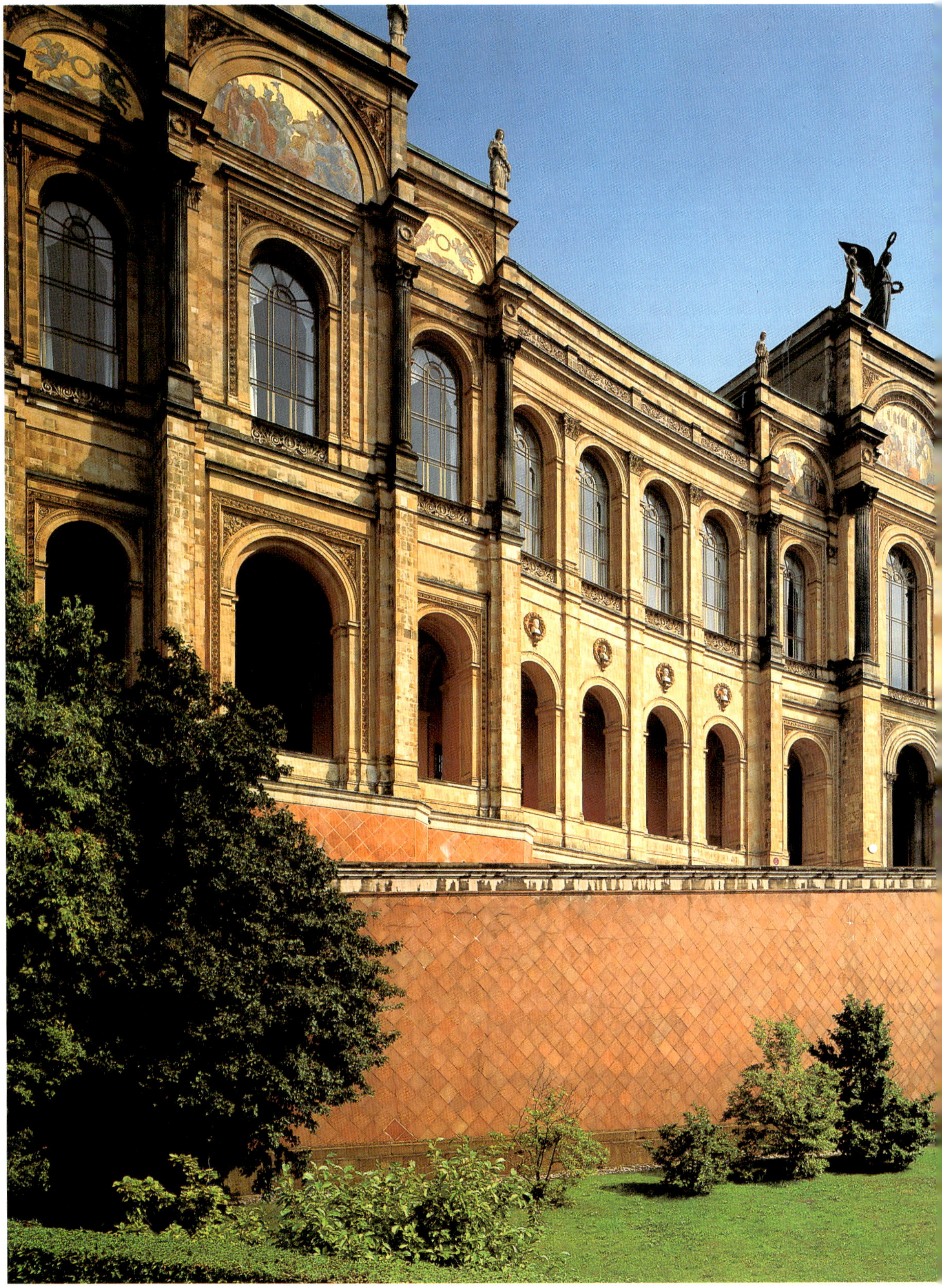

The show front of the Maximilianeum from the northwest

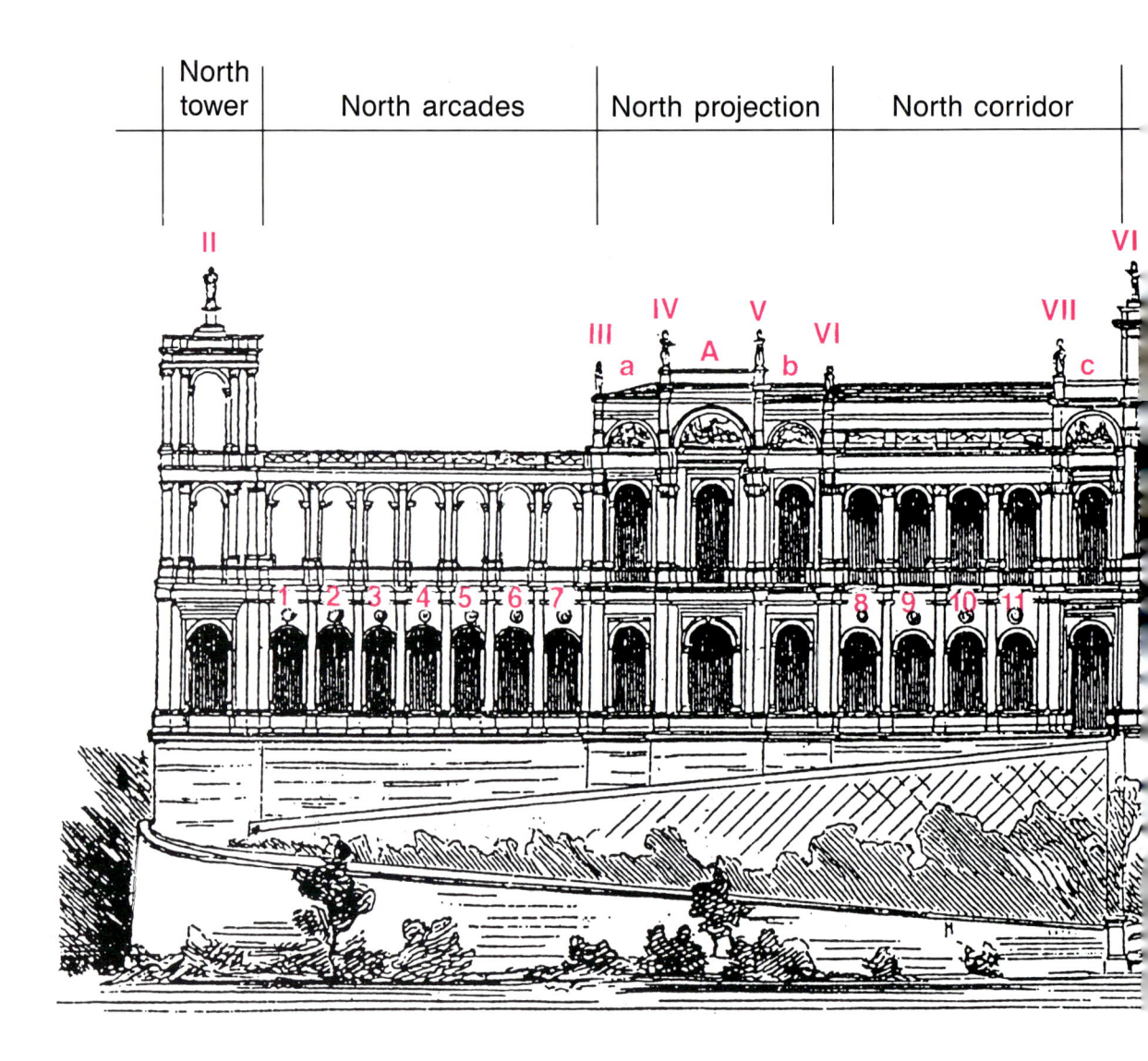

	North tower	North arcades	North projection	North corridor

Mosaics

A Domestic treaty of Pavia

   a
   b   Aids of the sciences

B The endowment of Ettal

   c Singers' competition at the Wartburg
   d Opening of the University of Ingolstadt

C Liberation of Vienna from the Turks

   e
   f   Trophies of war

Figures

I	Nike
II – VII	Victories with garlands
VIII, IX	Victories with palm branches
X – XV	Victories with garlands

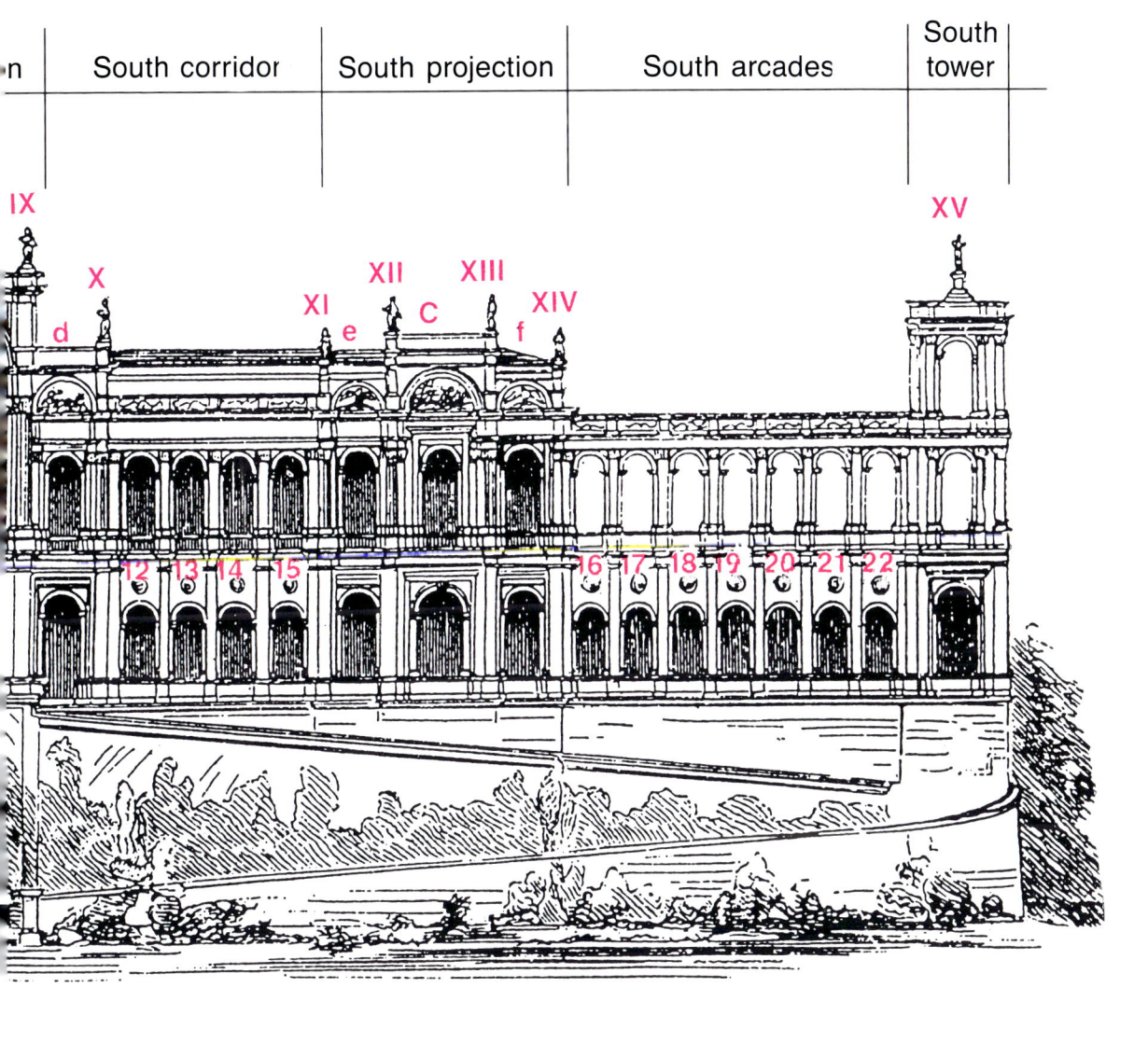

	South corridor	South projection	South arcades	South tower

Busts

- 1 Francis of Assisi
- 2 Gregory the Great
- 3 Vinzent de Paul
- 4 Socrates
- 5 Confuzius
- 6 Cicero
- 7 Leibniz
- 8 Archimedes
- 9 Brutus
- 10 Demosthenes
- 11 Homer
- 12 Gustavus Adolphus
- 13 Caesar
- 14 Hannibal
- 15 Alexander the Great
- 16 Sappho
- 17 Plato
- 18 Solon
- 19 Lycurgus
- 20 Aristotle
- 21 Pericles
- 22 Pythagoras

Singers' competition at the Wartburg. Mosaic on the centre projection

Karl Theodor von Piloty: Singer's competition at the Wartburg, oil sketch in the reading room

Foundation of the University of Ingolstadt by duke Ludwig IX the Rich in 1472. Mosaic on the centre projection

Foundation of Ettal Monastery by Emperor Ludwig IV the Bavarian in 1330. Mosaic on the centre projection

Liberation of Vienna form the Turks in 1683. Mosaic on the southern projection

Domestic treaty entered into by Emperor Ludwig IV the Bavarian at Pavia in 1329. Mosaic on the northern projection

Michael Echter: Wittelsbach Domestic Treaty of Pavia, oil sketch for the painting on the west façade, now in the 1st floor of the main building

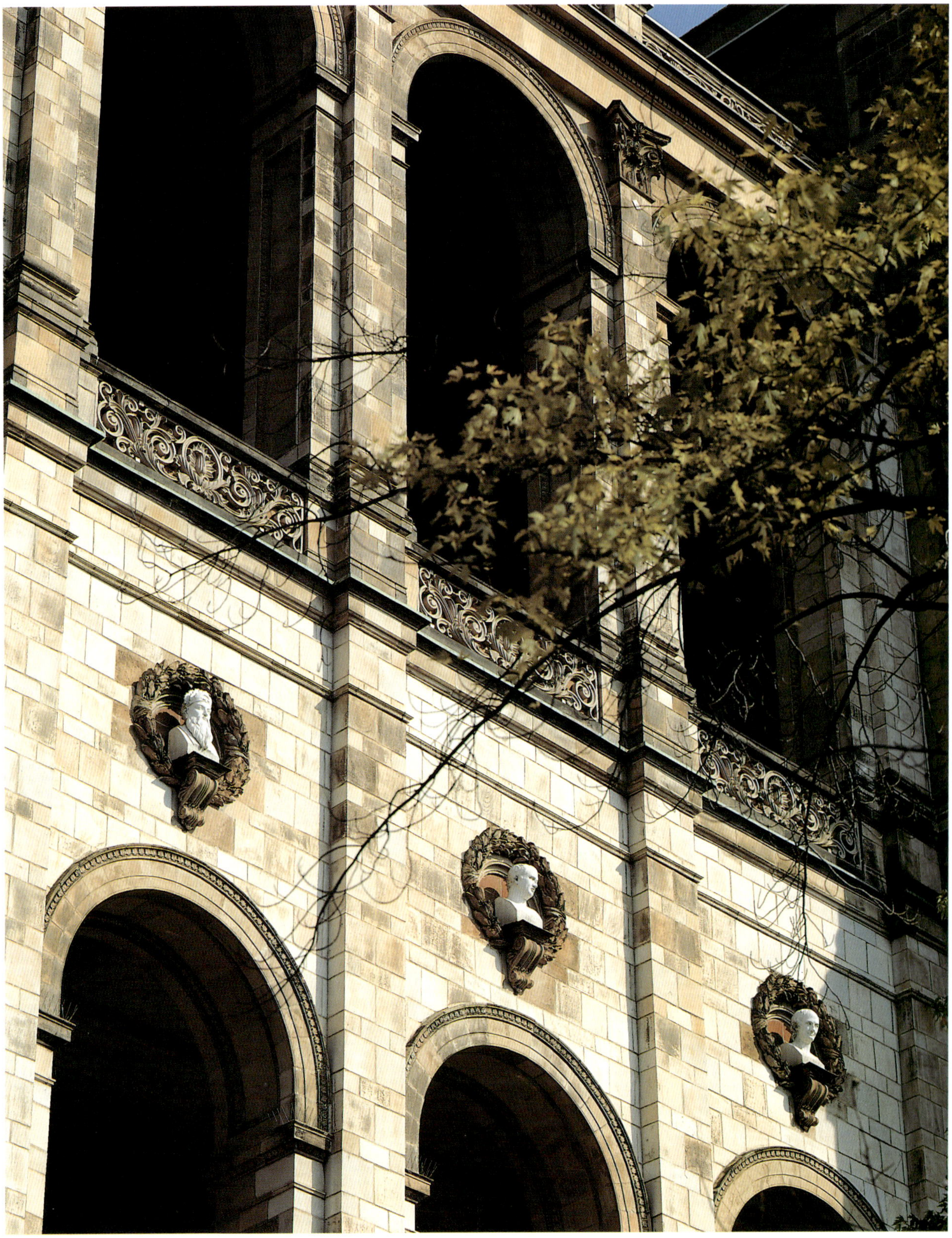

The mosaics on the northern projection – after Michael Echter (1812–1879), one of the first and most important illustrators of Wagner's music – depict the domestic treaty between Emperor Ludwig IV of Bavaria and his two nephews at Pavia in 1329 as a model of statesmanlike achievement; the aids of the sciences shown at both sides (globe, books) refer to the cycle of frescoes in the hall beneath. The counterpart on the southern projection – after the painter of battle scenes Feodor Dietz (1813–1870) – presents the liberation of Vienna from the Turks in 1683 under the leadership of Duke Charles of Lorraine, the King of Poland Johann III Sobieski and Elector Max Emanuel of Bavaria as a noteworthy attainment of the art of war; the associated trophies of war at both sides again refer to the pictorial programme of the room situated here. The 22 laurel-wreathed busts over the lower row of arcades, like the 24 marble busts by Peter Schöpf and Johann von Halbig which originally stood in the colonnades above, represent "benefactors, inventors, sages, men of literature, statesmen and military commanders" (at the north: from Homer to St. Francis of Assisi, at the south: from Gustavus II Adolphus to Pythagoras); when the façade was renovated in 1962/63, three of them had to be replaced, and at the same time a bust of the Greek poetess Sappho by the sculptor Scheerbaum was added.

Connected to the ostentatious public building of the Maximilianeum at the east surrounding the staircase is a five-storey rectangular building, whose simplicity marks it as the *back* of the display façade. Here there were once (and to some extent they still remain) rooms for the purpose of accommodation and teaching, sick rooms, refectories, conversation rooms, library and reading rooms and halls for gymnastics, fencing and dancing for the scholarship foundation and the royal Pagerie, and also the living quarters of the directors of both institutions. In the first storey the offices of the President and the Director of the Bavarian Landtag and parliamentary chambers are now accommodated. Connecting sections lead from the east corridors to the modern extension buildings, which are of the same height, and the lower annexed rooms at the north and south ends.

◁ *Detail of the west façade with the busts of Confucius, Cicero and Leibniz*

Late Gothic crucifix in the staircase

The Interior and its Furnishings

If the visitor enters the Maximilianeum through the main portal at the west, he will find himself in a *vestibule* surrounded by pillared arcades; in place of the present flat ceiling there was once shallow barrel vaulting here. The side corridors are five steps higher and lead to the "permanent exhibition" on the Bavarian Parliament for visitors and the Post Office 85 to the south, and to the Landtag restaurant with its garden room, the Maximilian, Bürklein and Bavaria rooms to the north. If one looks up the *staircase,* one's attention is caught by a monumental Late Gothic crucifix from Chieming near Traunstein (c. 1520; on permanent loan from the Bavarian National Museum) in the

67 *View of the staircase from the vestibule*

gallery. Halfway up, where the busts of the four Graeco-Roman statesmen and theoreticians Solon, Plato, Demosthenes and Cicero, originally part of the cycle which stood in the colonnades, have been displayed since 1992, the staircase divides into 2 sections which lead to the open arcades of the Stone Hall. If one looks around before entering this, one will see in the tympanums of the blind arcades the sgraffito cycle by Engelbert Seibertz (1813–1905), the Westphalian painter and holder of the Maximilian Order, which was completed in 1872 and is now fragmentary; its original nine allegories were: "teaching, peace, diligence – education, piety, justice/lawfulness – courage, patriotism, danger".

Ground plan of the first upper storey

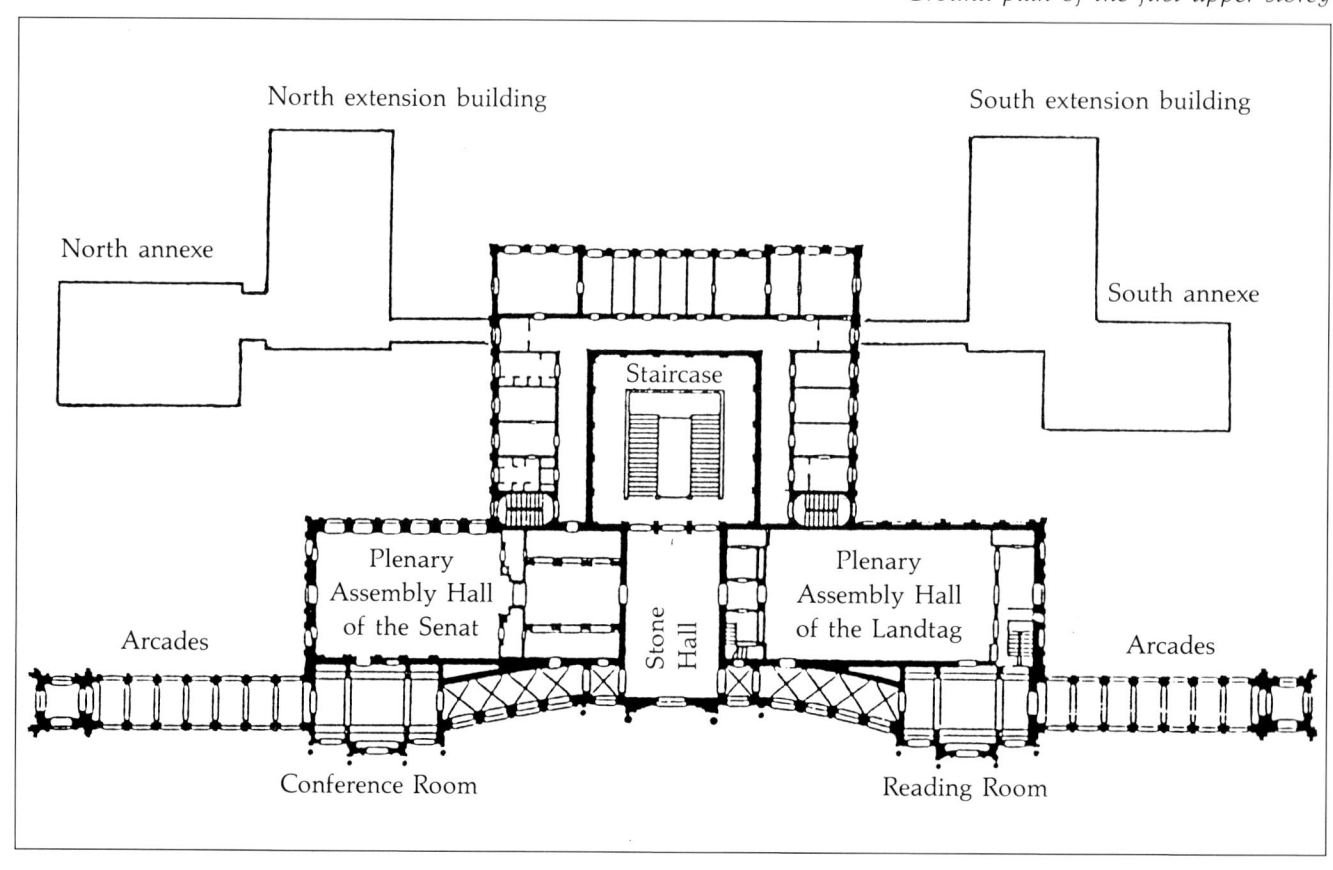

69　*Staircase gallery*

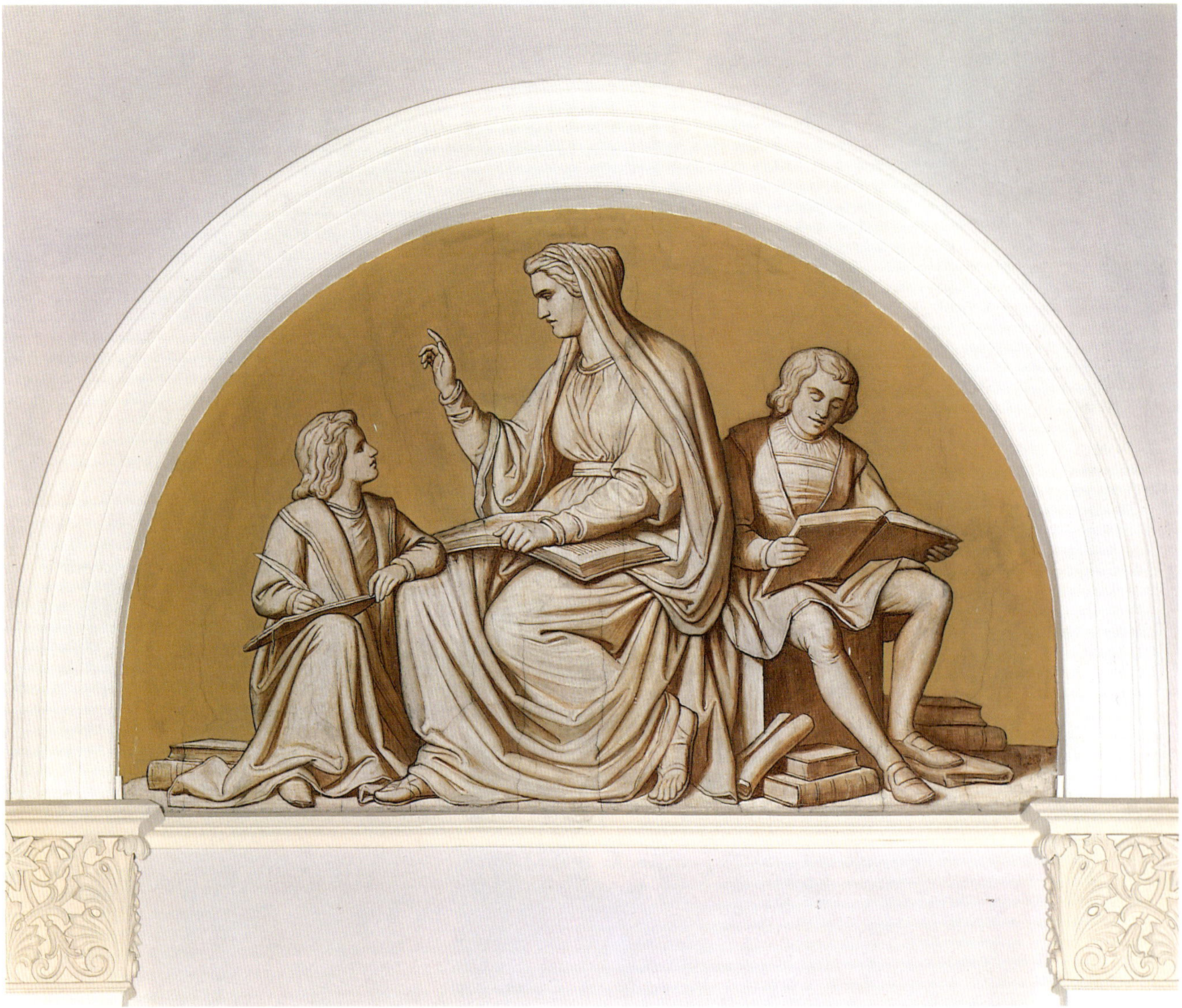

Engelbert Seibertz: Teaching and Justice, sgraffiti in the staircase

(Illus. p. 72, 73:) Peter Schöpf and Johann von Halbig: Demosthenes, Solon – Cicero, Plato, marble busts in the staircase

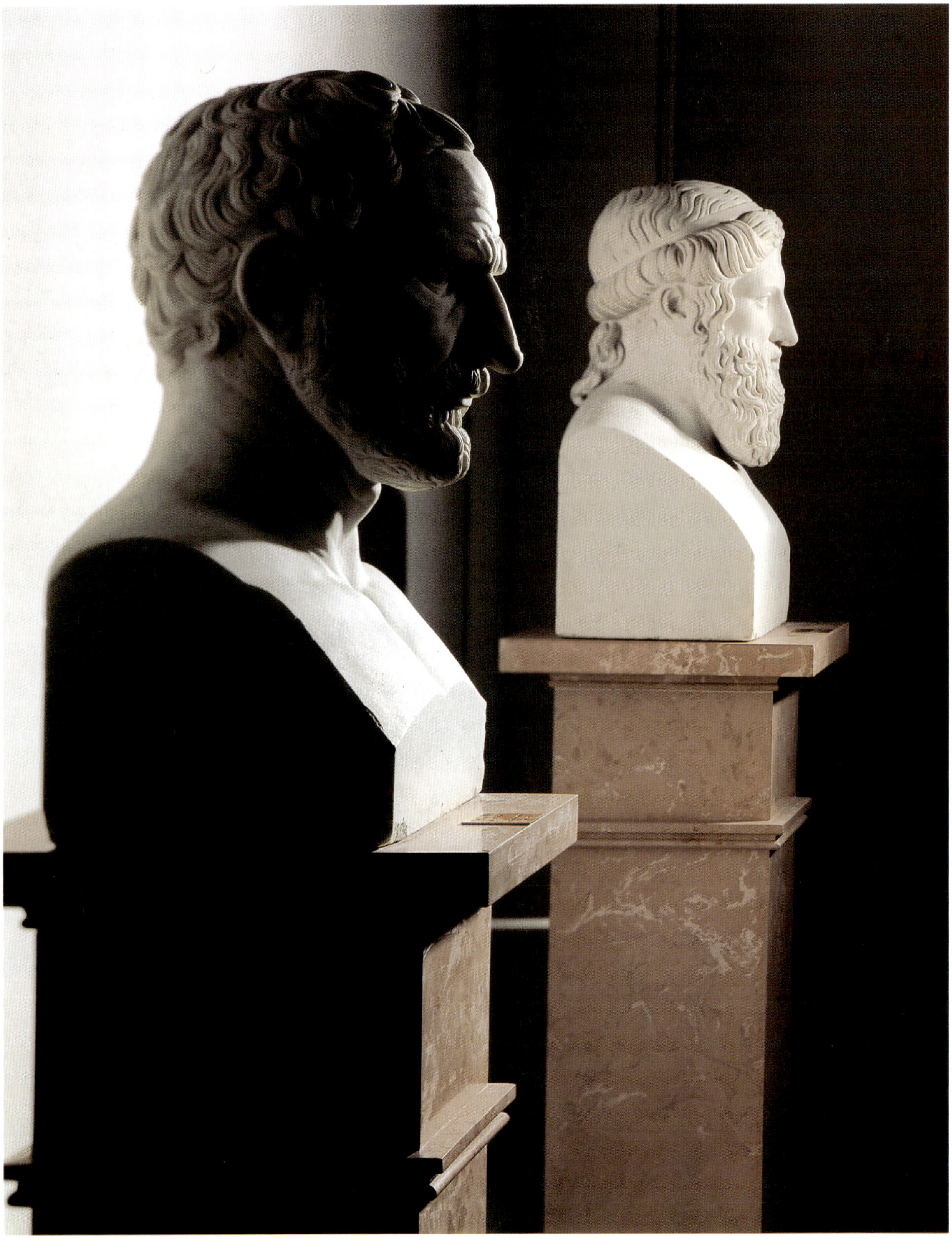

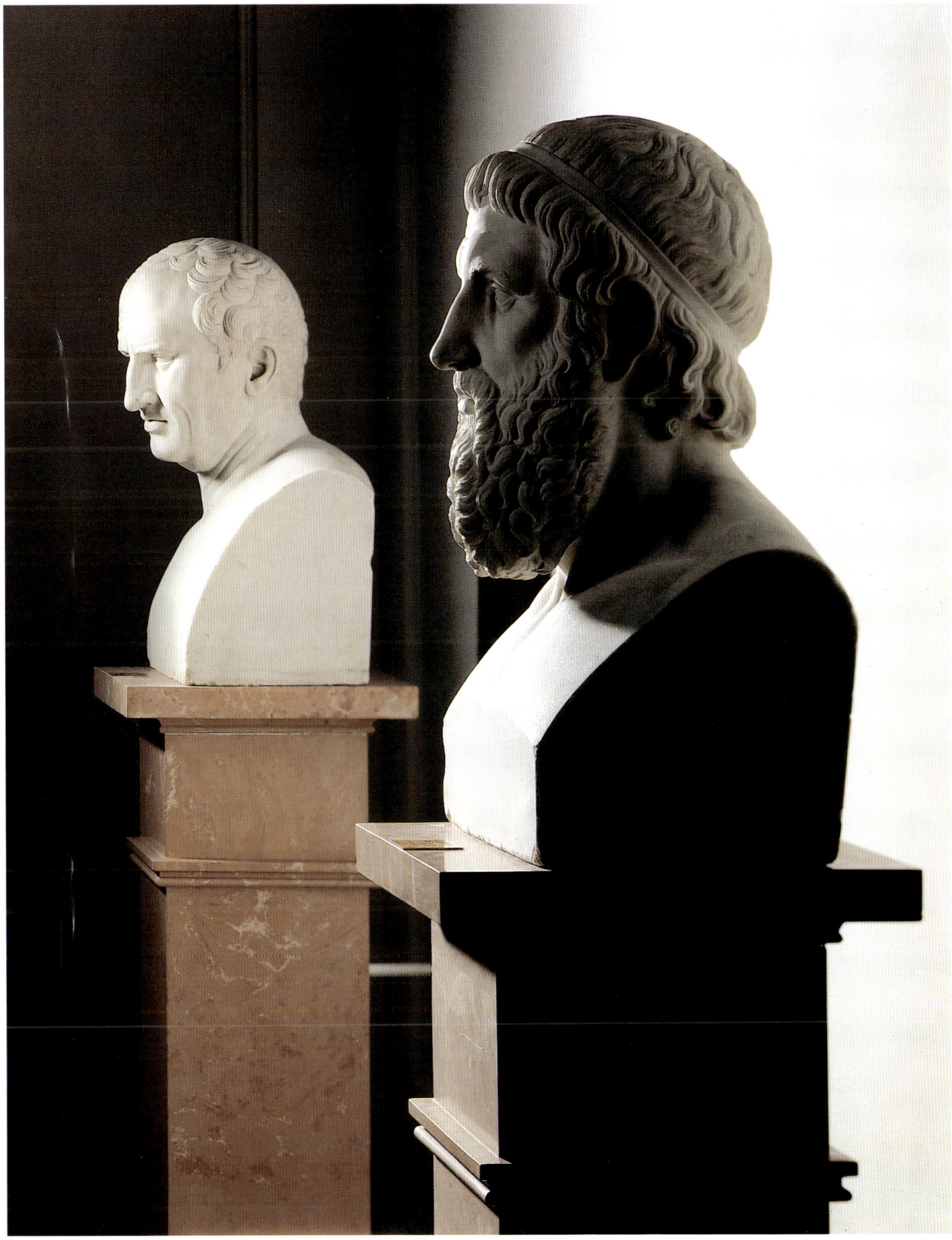

Maximilian room in the Landtag restaurant

Oriel in the Maximilian room in the Landtag restaurant ▷

75

Eckard Hauser: Bavarian Alpine Foothills, wall painting in the garden room of the Landtag restaurant

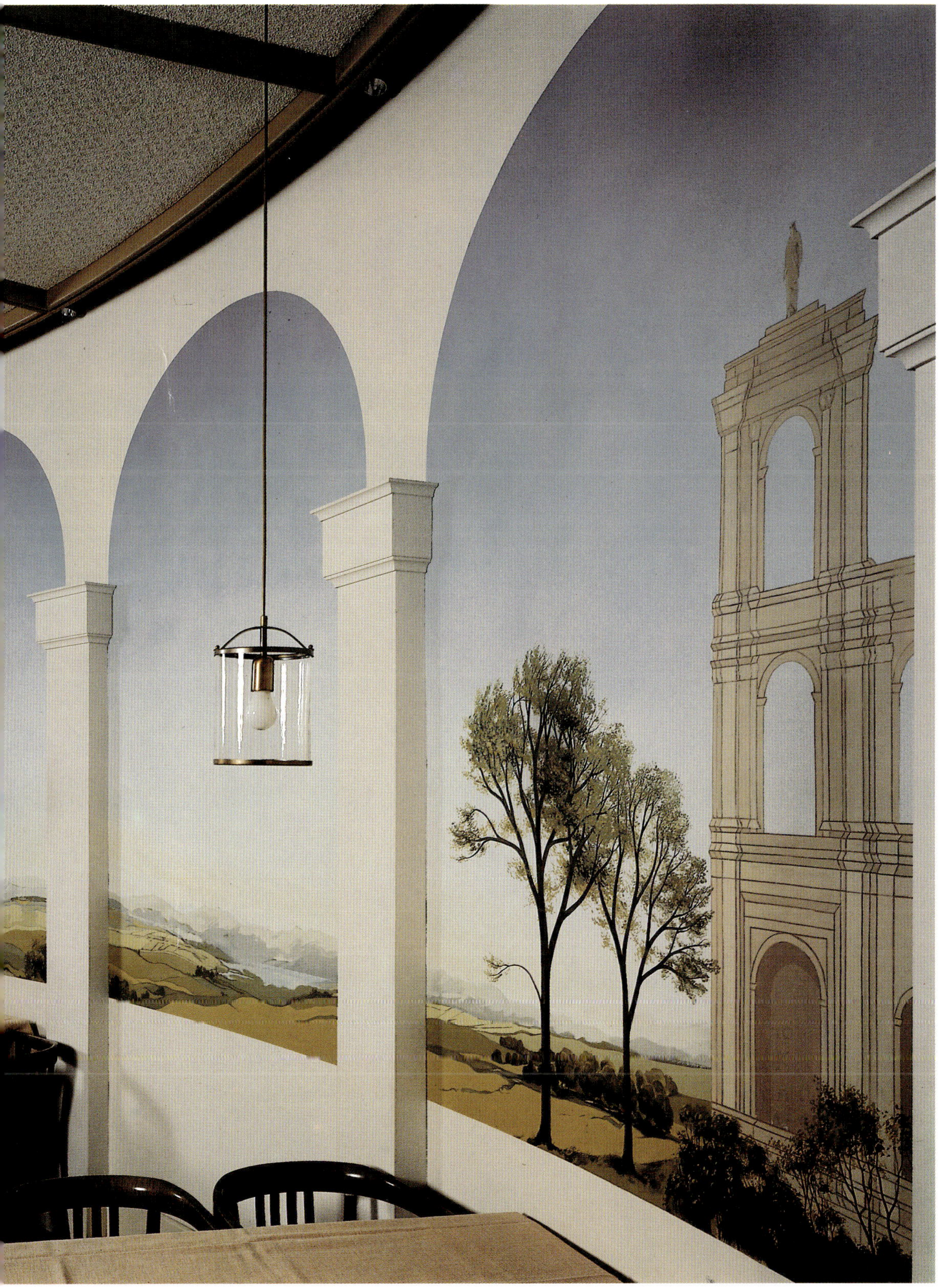

Bürklein room in the Landtag restaurant

Bavarian room in the Landtag restaurant

Edmund Harburger: Inn lounge in Schaftlach, painting in the Bavarian room of the Landtag restaurant

Karl Ludwig Seeger: Preparing for the Procession, painting in the Landtag President's office

View of the Maximilianeum from free balloon, xylograph (after a painting by Theodor Pixis) in the Bürklein room

Tausend Meter über München.

83 *Josef Wackerle: Ganymede, majolica statue in the passage connecting the main building to the northern annexe*

On the side walls of the *Stone Hall*, named after the reception and ceremonial hall of Nymphenburg Castle, there hang two huge paintings on canvas dating from 1861 and 1859: at the south "The Coronation of Emperor Charlemagne in 800" by the Hanoverian court painter Friedrich Kaulbach (1822–1903) and at the north "The Coronation of Emperor Ludwig IV the Bavarian in 1328" by August von Kreling (1819–1876), the Director of the Nuremberg Kunstgewerbeschule (college of applied art). They are the remnants of a work commissioned by King Max II which once comprised 30 oil paintings, showing events of world history (from the Fall to the Battle of Nations at Leipzig), intended to educate the people and encourage the painting of historical scenes; the western rooms of the first floor of the Maximilianeum were reserved vor them.

August von Kreling: The Coronation of Ludwig the Bavarian, painting in the Stone Hall

◁ *Friedrich Kaulbach: The Coronation of Charlemagne, painting in the Stone Hall*

The south-eastern of the four rectangular portals in the Stone Hall is distinguished by an oak door, with strongly three-dimensional reliefs (personifications of the foundations of a community), made in 1949 by the Vereinigte Werkstätten. It leads to the *Plenary Assembly Hall of the Bavarian Landtag* with the benches of the 204 representatives arranged in a semi-circle and the podiums for visitors and press at the sides. On the front wall behind the seat of the President of the Landtag and the armchairs of the members of the government of the Free State of Bavaria hangs a splendid tapestry designed by Professor Hermann Kaspar with the Great Bavarian State Coat of Arms (consisting of the lion of the Palatinate, the Franconian rake, the blue panther of Old Bavaria, the three Hohenstaufen lions of Swabia, the Bavarian lozenges on a heart-shaped shield and the so-called People's Crown) held by two lions, and the coats of arms of the government cities of Bavaria (of which there were eight until 1945; from the left: Augsburg, Munich, Regensburg, Würzburg, Landshut, Bayreuth, Speyer and Ansbach). At both sides of the tapestry, round stone reliefs are placed as maxims in view of the Landtag members, with the busts of the personifications of "Justice" and "planning with foresight". Opposite, the naval battle between the Greeks and the Persians at Salamis mentioned above can be seen in full progress in the painting by Wilhelm von Kaulbach. (During the plenary assembly meetings, the oil painting, which measures c. 5 by 9 m, is covered by a fire-protection curtain.)

The north-eastern portal forms the entry to the *Full assembly hall of the Bavarian Senate*. The bronze reliefs on the sconces, also by the Vereinigte Werkstätten, show Bavaria and Europe on each side of the seat of the President of the Senate and elsewhere classical gods and mythological figures referring to the ten corporations represented in the Senate.

The north-western portal of the Stone Hall open into the northern corridor, the so-called *President's Corridor*, which follows the curve of the façade. It is named after the portraits of previous Landtag Presidents which hang here: Dr. Michael Horlacher (1946–1950), Dr. h.c. Georg Stang (1950/51), Dr. Dr. Alois Hundhammer (1951–1954), Dr. Hans Ehard (1954–1960), Rudolf Hanauer (1960–1978) and Dr. Franz Heubl (1978–1990).

Oak doors leading to the Plenary Assembly Hall of the Bavarian Landtag ▷

87

Clock in the Plenary Assembly Hall of the Bavarian Landtag

Hermann Kaspar: Great Bavarian State Coat of Arms, tapestry in the Plenary Assembly Hall of the Bavarian Landtag

90

Planning with Foresight and Justice, stone busts in the Plenary Assembly Hall of the Bavarian Landtag (signed "Ffq E")

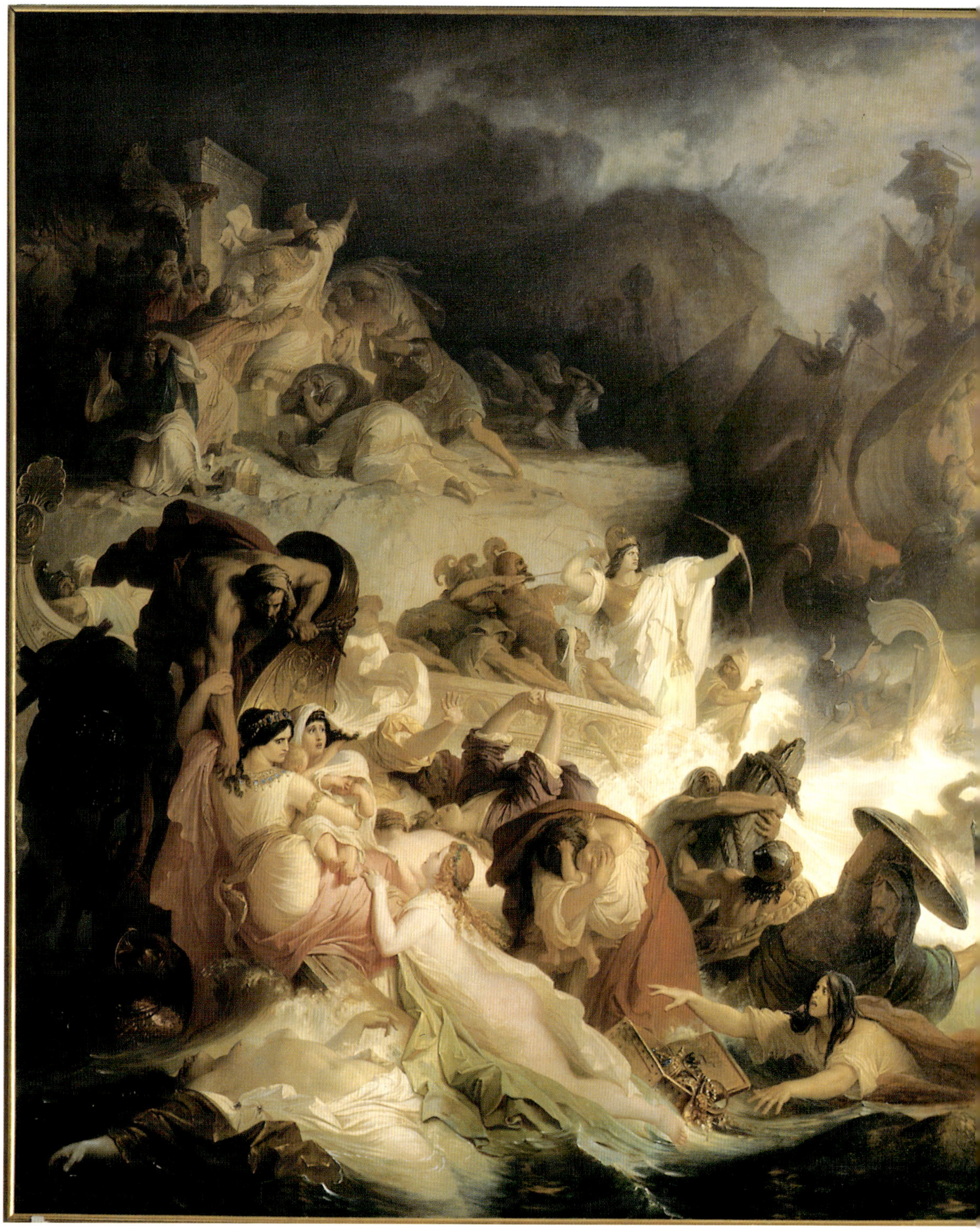

Wilhelm von Kaulbach: The Naval Battle of Salamis, painting in the Plenary Assembly Hall of the Bavarian Landtag

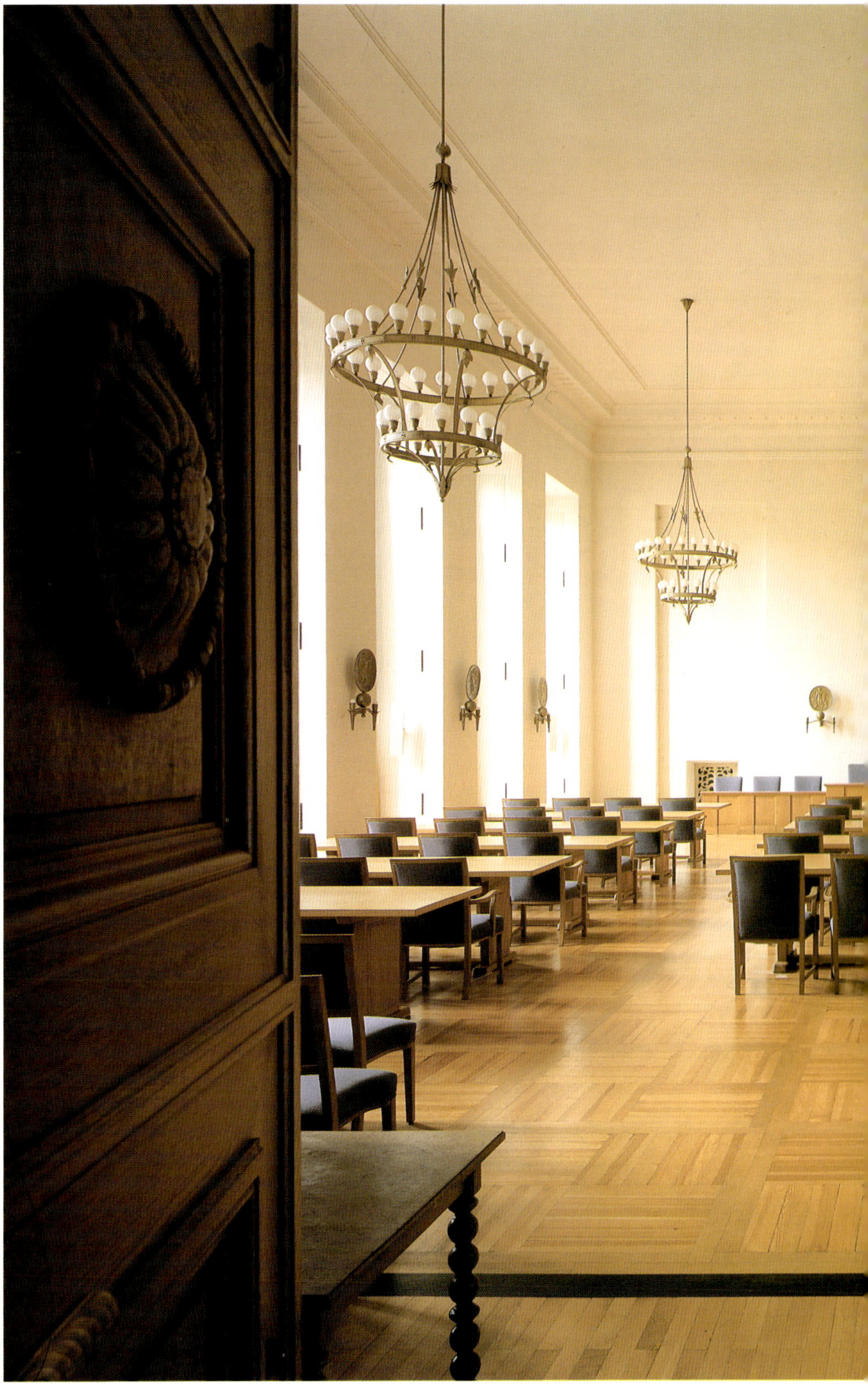

Plenary Assembly Hall of the
Bavarian Senate

R. Kommer: President of the Landtag Dr. Michael Horlacher, painting in the President's Corridor

R. Kommer: President of the Landtag Dr. Georg Stang, painting in the President's Corridor

Ernst Müller-Gräfe: President of the Landtag Dr. Dr. Alois Hundhammer, painting in the President's Corridor

Hans Jakob Mann: President of the Landtag Dr. Hans Ehard, painting in the president's Corridor

Magda Bittner-Simmet: President of the Landtag Rudolf Hanauer, painting in the President's Corridor

Toni Oberniedermayr: President of the Landtag Dr. Franz Heubl, painting in the President's Corridor

The corridor leads into what is now the *Conference Room*, which is used for ceremonial receptions and meetings of the Council of Elders of the Landtag. The rectangular hall is divided into three bays: the large central area, distinguished by four marble columns giving the impression of a canopy and two narrower bays to the south and the north. The east wall of the central area is filled by a fresco by Engelbert Seibertz showing the Maximilianeum in February 1864, before the change of design, with pointed arches and neo-Gothic windows (the oil sketch for this picture is dated "1858"). It shows the imaginary introduction of Alexander von Humboldt into a circle of famous men of the arts and sciences in Bavaria. The natural scientist is being introduced by the Presidents of the two Bavarian Academies under Max II: the chemist Justus von Liebig (Academy of Sciences) and the painter of historical scenes Wilhelm von Kaulbach (Academy of Visual Arts). In a semicircle the following are gathered: (from left) the theologian Ignaz von Döllinger, the political economist Friedrich von Hermann, the architect Leo von Klenze, the optician Josef von Fraunhofer, the historian Lorenz von Westenrieder, the lawyer Johann Georg von Lori, the philologist Friedrich von Thiersch, the philosopher Friedrich Wilhelm von Schelling, the geographer Carl Ritter (accompanying Humboldt), the historian and statesman Wilhelm von Doenniges (who devised the pictorial programme of the "historical gallery") and his teacher Leopold von Ranke, the poet Emmanuel Geibel, the sculptor Ludwig von Schwanthaler, the writer Count August von Platen-Hallermünde, the Musical Director Franz Lacher (who composed the ceremonial anthem on the occasion of the laying of the foundation stone), the philosopher Franz Xaver von Baader and the mineralogist Franz von Kobell; those of the group who were already deceased are shown in the background. The painting is complemented by the allegory of "Truth" (with the mirror) between "Chemistry" and "Architecture" in the tympanums on the same side. On the other walls of the conference room are the series of portraits painted by Georg Hiltensperger (1806–1890) of six "benefactors" (starting at the northwest: Bartolomé de Las Casas, the apostle to the Indians; Duke Leopold von Braunschweig-Lüneburg, who was drowned in the attempt to aid the inhabitants of Frankfurt on the Oder when the dam broke; Jakob Fugger the Rich, the founder of the Fuggerei in Augsburg; William Penn, the founder of the Quaker state of Pennsylvania with its liberal constitution, religious tolerance and good neighbourly relationships with the American Indians; the Duke of Bavaria Wilhelm V the Pious, who supported the Jesuits in Bavaria and sponsored their missionary activities in China and Japan; Prince Bishop Julius Echter von Mespelbrunn, the founder of the Julius-Spital and the University in Würzburg) and six "inventors" (continuing south of the Seibertz fresco: Christopher Columbus, the discoverer of America; Johannes Gutenberg, who invented printing; Roger Bacon, 13th-century theologian and natural philosopher, who anticipated

Julius Zimmermann: King Max II of Bavaria, painting in the south corridor

many inventions of the age of technology; Nicolaus Copernicus, the discoverer of the heliocentric universe; James Watt, who invented the steam engine; Alois Senefelder, who invented lithography).

These paintings were intended to supplement of the already mentioned cycle of busts, which once extended along the whole length of the present President's Corridor and its continuation in the *Corridor south of the Stone Hall* as in a "Hall of Fame". Today the full-figure portrait of the young King Max II by Julius Zimmermann (1824–1906) hangs here, a copy after W. V. Kaulbach and on loan from the Bavarian State Painting Collections.

Conference room

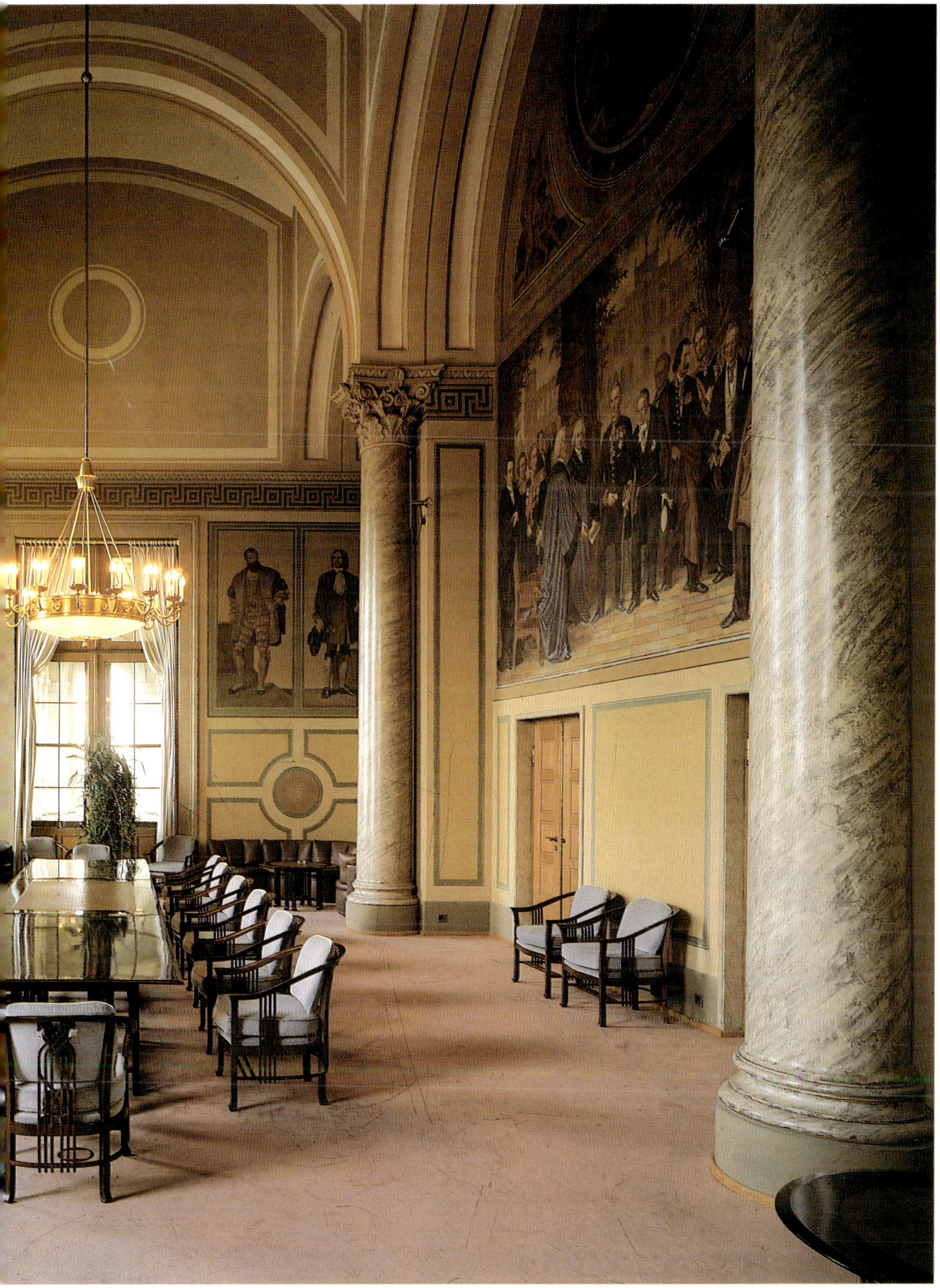

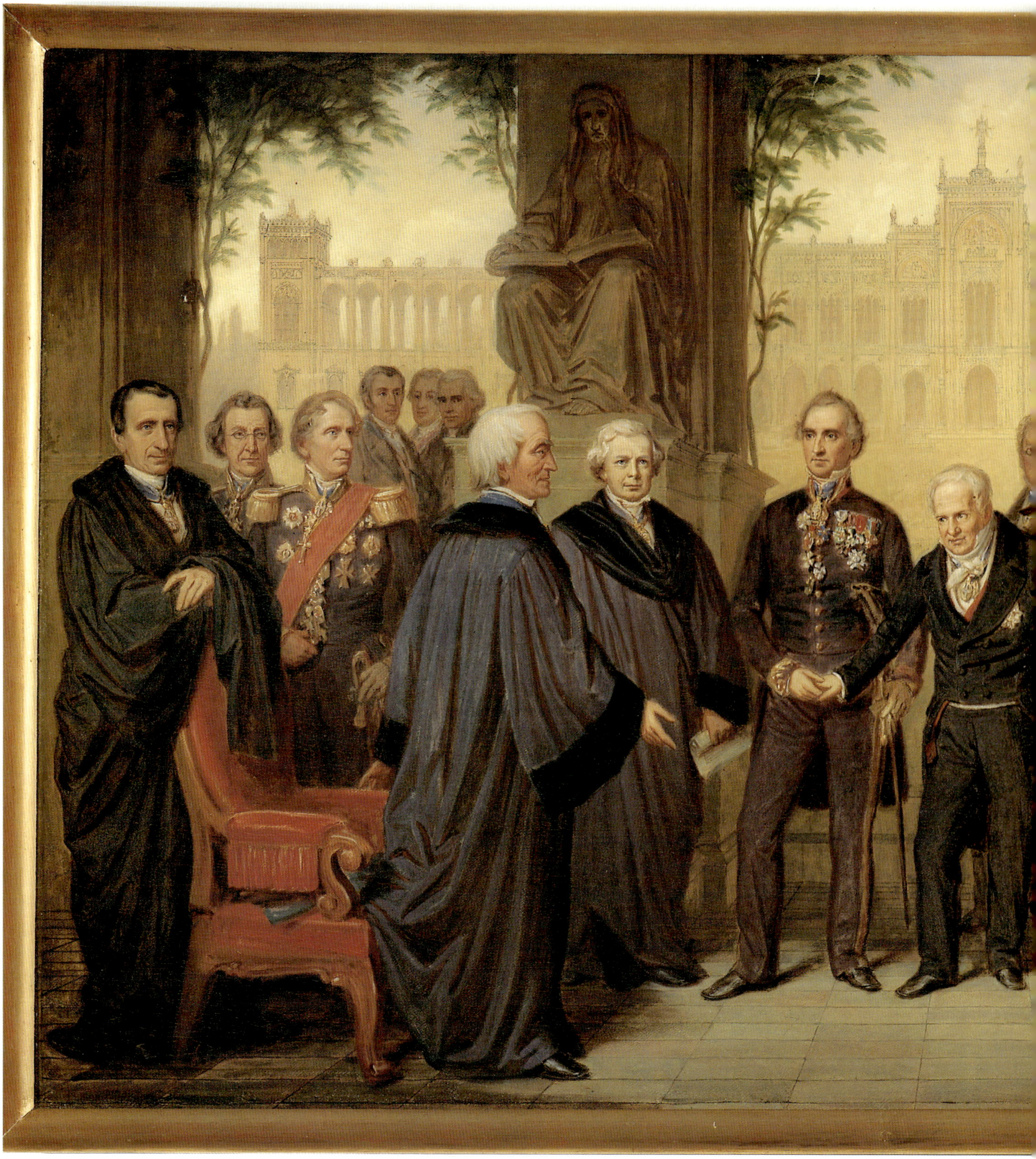

Engelbert Seibertz: The Introduction of Alexander von Humboldt, painting in the study foundation. Oil sketch for the wall painting in the conference room

Georg Hiltensperger: Jakob Fugger the Rich, William Penn. Wall paintings in the conference room

Georg Hiltensperger: Bartolomé de Las Casas, Duke Leopold von Braunschweig-Lüneburg. Wall ▷
paintings in the conference room

109

Georg Hiltensperger: Duke Wilhelm V. of Bavarian and Prince Bishop Julius Echter von Mespelbrunn. Wall paintings in the conference room

Georg Hiltensperger: Christopher Columbus, Johannes Gutenberg. Wall paintings in the conferece room

111

Georg Hiltensperger: Roger Bacon, Nicolaus Copernicus. Wall paintings in the conference room

113 *Georg Hiltensperger: James Watt and Alois Senefelder. Wall paintings in the conference room*

114

The adjoining room, which serves as a *reading room* for the representatives, is the counterpart to the conference room in its situation, shape and pictorial programme, but in contrast to the latter it displays a more elegant colouring scheme (shimmering gold framing the panels, black marble pillar columns) and pointed arches, which show that the shell of the Maximilianeum (apart from the arcades and the wings) was complete when the King died in 1864. The wall frescoes by E. Seibertz on the east side of the reading room have been lost: in the centre a meeting of important statesmen at the time of the Congress of Vienna was portrayed (Prince Talleyrand/France, Count Montgelas/Bavaria, Prince Hardenberg/Prussia, Prince Metternich/Austria and Hofrat von Gentz in the background as keeper of the minutes); in the tympanums is the Goddess of Peace, History with the auxiliary sciences of Geography and Archaeology together with the Fury of War. In its place, above the entrance to the plenary assembly hall of the Landtag, there hangs today K. V. Piloty's oil sketch on which the painting of the singers' competition at the Wartburg (cf. west façade) is based. The portraits by Friedrich Pecht (1814–1903), the painter of historical scenes, dated 1868, represent "six generals" (beginning at the northwest: the Russian General Alexander von Suvorov, the Austrian Field Marshal Archduke Karl, the Prussian Field Marshal Gebhard von Blücher and the British Field Marshal Arthur Wellesley, Duke of Wellington, who all achieved victories over France during the Napoleonic era; their antagonist Emperor Napoleon I; Frederick II the Great, King of Prussia) and six "statesmen" (continuing in the same sequence: William I of Orange; the Swedish King Gustavus I Vasa; the two French ministers Richelieu and Sully; King Alfred of England and his continental equivalent, Emperor Charlemagne).

If the visitor casts a final glance through the window, he will realize something of the vision which was expressed as follows by the Bavarian Chief Minister Ludwig von der Pfordten on the occasion of the laying of the foundation stone of the building in 1857: "Thus its inhabitants, undisturbed by the noise of the streets, will yet find themselves in close proximity to the capital. Their eyes will rest daily on the scene of the glorious history of their fatherland, just as the inner halls of the Maximilianeum shall show ... the most important deeds of world history to their spirits in the form of great paintings".

◁ *Pointed arch in the reading room*

KARDINAL RICHELIEU   HERZOG SULLY

Reading room

Engelbert Seibertz: Gathering of important statesmen at the time of the Vienna congress. Painting in the study foundation, sketch of the destroyed fresco in the reading room. The centre group of figures shows (from left to right) Prince Talleyrand, France; Count Montgelas, Bavaria; Prince Hardenberg, Prussia; Prince Metternich, Austria; and Hofrat von Gentz

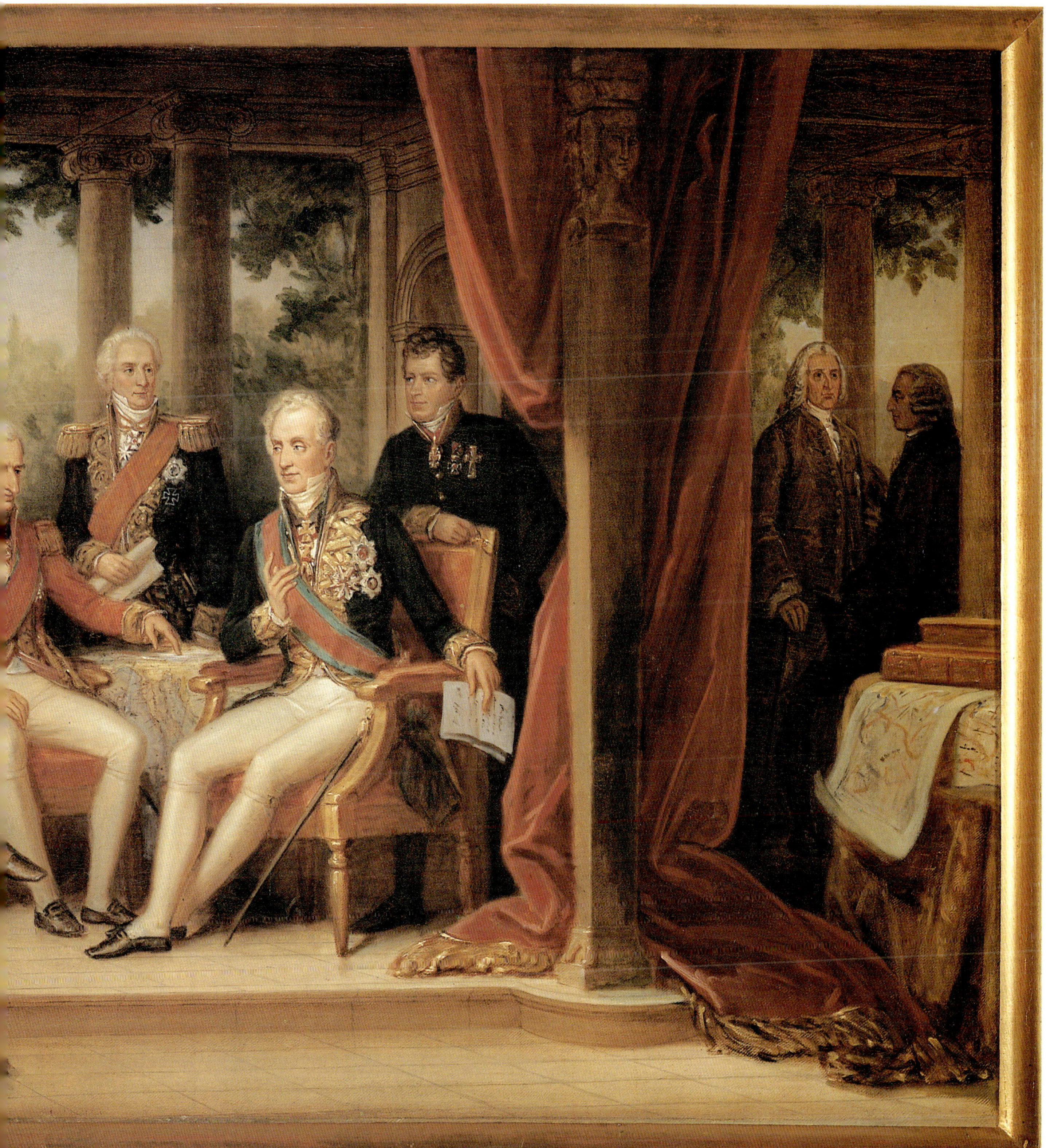

Friedrich Pecht: Alexander von Suvarov, Archduke Karl of Austria. Wall paintings in the reading room

GEBHARDT v. BLÜCHER. **ARTHUR WELLINGTON.**

121 *Friedrich Pecht: Gebhardt von Blücher, Arthur Wellesley Duke of Wellington. Wall paintings in the reading room*

NAPOLEON I BONAPARTE.   FRIEDERICH II D. GR:

Friedrich Pecht: Napoleon I, Frederick the Great. Wall paintings in the reading room

123   *Friedrich Pecht: William I of Orange, Gustavus I Vasa. Wall paintings in the reading room*

KARDINAL RICHELIEU. **HERZOG SULLY.**

Friedrich Pecht: Cardinal Richelieu, Duke Sully. Wall paintings in the reading room

125 *Friedrich Pecht: King Alfred of England and Charlemagne. Wall paintings in the reading room*

Constitution of the Kingdom of Bavaria of 1818

The Bavarian Parliament

The History of the Bavarian Parliament

The Bavarian Landtag has its historical roots in the Bavarian *Land estates*, which were not as yet elected representatives of the people but representatives of the interests of the three leading social groups in the Land: the nobility, the clergy and the towns/markets. From their original function as advisers to the rulers of the Land they developed their various rights in the course of the Middle Ages: e.g. the right to participate in decisions on war and peace; the right to hold courts of inferior jurisdiction; the appropriation, levying and administration of taxes; complaints and opposition. In the Deed of Schnaitbach of 1302 and in the Ottonian Privileges of 1311 the Dukes of Bavaria first laid down the freedoms of the Land estates. At every accession of a new government, the Land estates paid homage to the new sovereign of the Land, after he had confirmed their current rights. They assembled at the Landtag convened by the sovereign from 1505 in the government cities of Straubing, Munich, Landshut and Ingolstadt, from the end of the 16th century onwards only in Munich. In the age of absolutism the Bavarian Electors from Max Emanuel onwards ceased to convene a Landtag. In its place, however, from 1669 on, a permanent committee, the so-called "Landschaftsverordnung", exercised the rights of the Landtag and increased its own number by electing further members. After the foundation of the Kingdom of Bavaria the Land estates were dissolved in 1808.

After the constitution of the Kingdom of Bavaria had come into force in 1818, an *Assembly of the Estates* was convened on 4th February 1819 for an electoral period of six years; it consisted of a chamber with 50 Reich councillors (princes of the royal dynasty, heads of the former ruling houses directly subordinate to the Emperor, representatives of the higher Catholic and Protestant clergy, the supreme crown officer and members appointed by the king) and a chamber of 115 representatives of five different classes, some of them elected directly and some indirectly (noblemen with rights to hold court, representatives of the universities, clergy, citizens as representatives of the towns and markets and landowners); the Presidents of the two chambers were appointed by the King. The constitution provided for five permanent committees: for legislation (which had only an advisory and approbative function), the discharge of state debts, taxes, complaints and general matters. Only a joint resolution of both chambers bound the government. The Assembly of the estates had its seat at no. 20 Prannerstrasse in Munich.

Since King Ludwig I did not accept the changes to the constitution called for by the assembly of the estates, he abdicated on 20th March 1848. His suc-

DIE KAMMER DER ABGEORDNETEN VO

Franz Hanfsteangl: The Chamber of Representatives, 1866

cessor, Max II, granted the *Landtag,* as the assembly was now called, the right to introduce legislation, ministerial accountability and a new electoral law, which was no longer based on a division into classes; from now on every taxpaying male citizen from the age of 25 had a right to vote; at the same time constituencies were introduced. In 1850 the first direct election of the President of the Chamber was held. From 1861 onwards political parties were formed in the chamber of representatives. In 1881 voting by secret ballot was achieved in the Landtag, and in 1906 direction election by the majority system. In 1912, the leader of the party was for the first time instructed to form a government.

On 8th November 1918, the Republic was proclaimed in Bavaria, and on 12th January 1919 the election of the *first sovereign Landtag* was held; women were now allowed to take part. The constitutional basis for this procedure was created on 14th August 1919. On 31st March 1933 the Gleichschaltung Law was passed and a new Landtag was appointed by the parties in accordance with the results of the last Reichtstag elections; this parliament – like the other German Land parliaments – was dissolved without replacement under the Reich Law of 30th January 1934. – After the catastrophe of the Second World War, the Bavarian people approved the constitution of the Free State of Bavaria on 1st December 1946 and at the same time elected the first *Bavarian Landtag,* which met at first in the Great Hall of the Ludwig-Maximilian University of Munich, later in the Brunnenhof Theatre in the Residence and the Sophie Hall of the Supreme Financial Office, until it found its final location in the Maximilianeum in January 1949.

Christian Steinicken: Seat of the Bavarian Landtag in Munich (Prannerstraße 20), watercolour, 1884

The Bavarian Landtag

Article 13 of the constitution of the Free State of Bavaria provides as follows: "The Landtag consists of the representatives of the Bavarian people. The Landtag members represent the people, not just one party. They are responsible only to their own conscience and are not bound by instructions". Every Bavarian citizen aged 18 or more has the right to vote in the Landtag elections; candidates must have reached the age of 21. The elections are contested by the parties, which are organized groups of citizens of the Land and organized groups of voters, in order to enforce their political aims. Since 1990 there have been 104 Bavarian constituencies. These are normally identical with the Rural Districts and Self-Administered Towns, unless their electorate is considerably larger or smaller than the constituency norm of approximately 100,000 inhabitants. In each of these constituencies, a Landtag member is chosen by direct election. The other 100 members enter the Landtag by way of the constituency lists of the seven administrative regions: 32 from Upper Bavaria, 10 from Lower Bavaria, 9 from the Upper Palatinate, 10 from Upper Franconia, 14 from Middle Franconia, 11 from Lower Franconia and 14 from Swabia. The legislative period is four years.

The Landtag members form parliamentary parties according to their political affiliations. In 1946 the *seats in parliament* were divided between the following parties: CSU (Christlich-Soziale-Union – Christian Social Union), SPD (Sozialdemokratische Partei Deutschlands – Social Democratic Party of Germany), WAV (Wirtschaftliche Aufbauvereinigung – Association for Economic Recovery) and F.D.P. (Freie Demokratische Partei – Free Democratic Party). In 1950 the WAV no longer stood for election, but there were two additional parties: BP (Bayernpartei – Bavarian Party) and BHE (Block der Heimatvertriebenen und Entrechteten – Group of expellees and those who have been deprived of their rights); however, after its amalgamation with the Deutsche Partei (German Party) in 1962, the latter no longer succeeded in being represented in the Landtag. In 1966 only three parties had members in parliament: CSU, SPD and, on this one occasion only, NPD (Nationaldemokratische Partei Deutschlands – National Democratic Party of Germany). From the 7th to the 9th legislative period, the F.D.P. was the third party after CSU and SPD. In 1982 only CSU and SPD were represented. Since 1986 Die Grünen (The Green Party) has been represented, and since 1990 the F.D.P. has also returned to the Landtag. Thus in the 12th legislative period there are once again four parliamentary parties in the Landtag: CSU, SPD, Die Grünen and F.D.P. In 1973 the five-per cent threshold clause has been introduced, whereby a party can only be represented in the Landtag if it receives a minimum of five per cent of all votes in the whole of Bavaria.

Last session of the first electoral period from 1946–1950 under Dr. Georg Stang as president

In the constituting meeting at the beginning of a legislative period, the plenary assembly of the members elects the President of the Landtag, the two Vice-Presidents and the clerks. This *Presidium* prepares the Landtag budget and is the highest administrative authority for the employees of the Landtag Office. The President and Vice-Presidents, together with representatives of all the parliamentary parties, form the *Council of Elders*, which supports the President and draws up the agenda of the plenary assembly. The main part of the parliament's work is carried out in the *Plenary Assembly* of the members. The Plenary Assembly Hall is the place where bills are read and voted on, and also the forum for the supervision of the executive. It is here, too, that "Topical Hours", debates on interpellations and answers to oral questions to the government are held. It is a fundamental principle that the plenary meetings are open to the public.

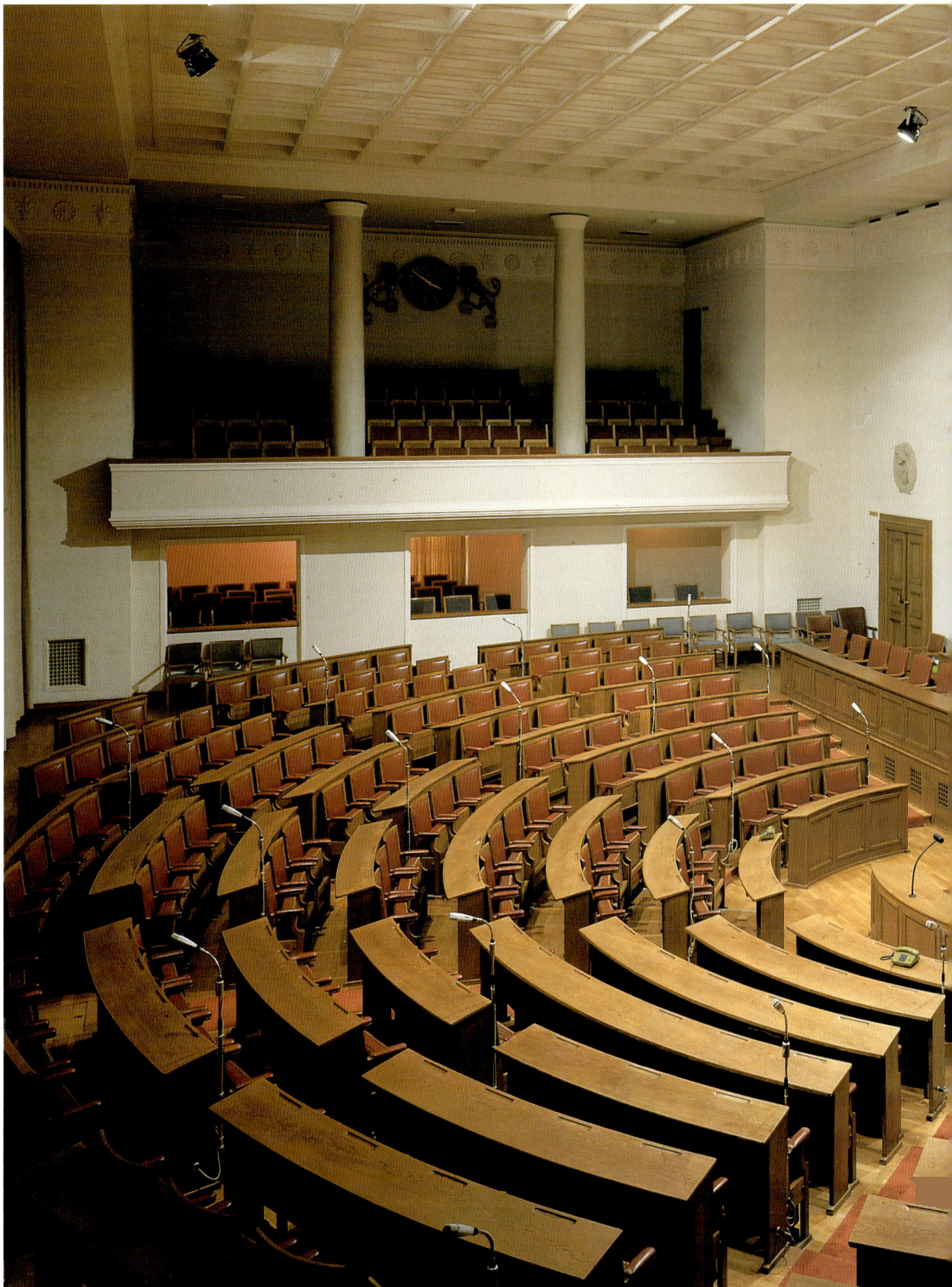

*Plenary Assembly Hall
of the Bavarian Landtag*

In contrast to the German Bundestag and other German Land parliaments, the sittings of the *committees* in Bavaria are also open to the public. The committees are composed of relevant experts from the parliamentary parties; they discuss bills and motions in detail and thus prepare the resolutions of the plenary assembly or decide on petitions from citizens. In the current 12th legislative period, there are also twelve standing committees: for standing orders and scrutiny of votes; for the Bavarian budget and financial questions; for constitutional, legal and communal questions; for economics and transport; for food, agriculture and forestry; for social, health and family policy; for questions of cultural policy; for questions relating to the civil service; for petitions and complaints; for federal and European matters; for domestic German development and questions relating to border areas; and for questions relating to the development of the Land and the environment. In addition, since 1990, there has been a Parliamentary Control Commission for the supervision of the activities of the Bavarian Office for the Protection of the Constitution. From time to time, Committees of Inquiry may also be appointed (up to now there have been 44 such committees). The Landtag determines the number of members of each committee, which is composed in proportion to the strength of the various parliamentary parties.

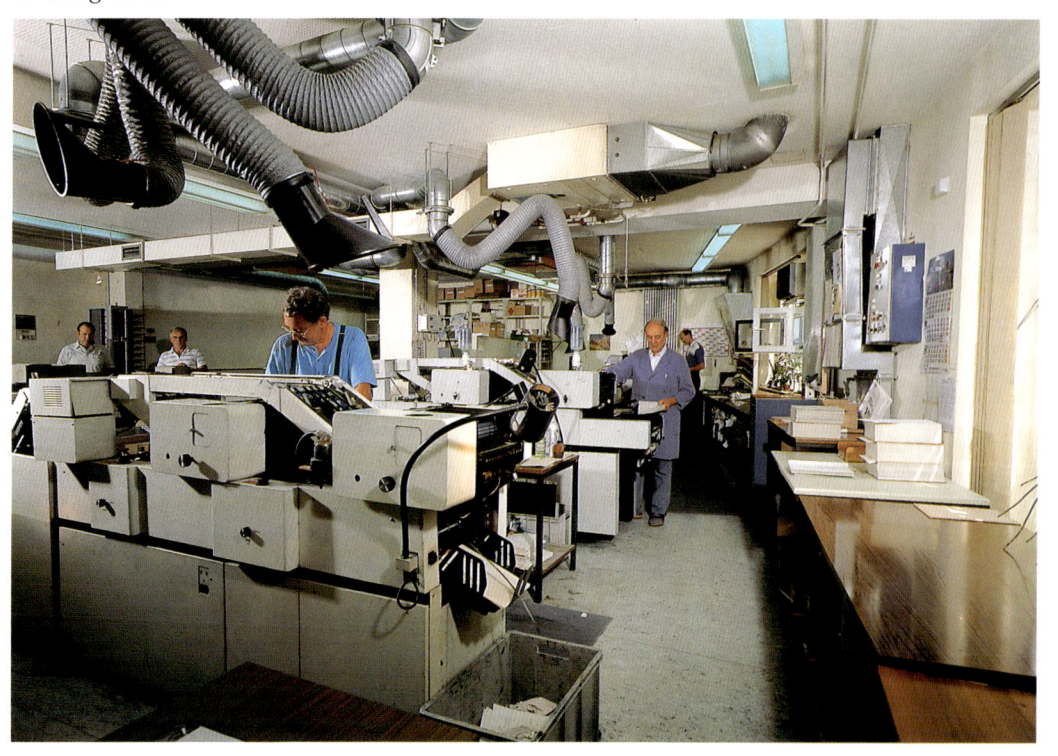

Printing room

Visitors' podium in the Plenary Assembly Hall of the Bavarian Landtag

To help him in conducting the business of the Landtag, the Landtag President has at his disposal the *Landtag Office* under the direction of the Landtag Director. Three departments are concerned with doing the necessary groundwork for the use of the Landtag members and fulfilling the many and various tasks which arise from running a modern parliament: "Parliamentary Service", "Public Relations and Information" and "Personnel, Administration and Documentation". The "Parliamentary Service" Department is responsible for preparing plenary and committee sittings, dealing with the administrative technicalities of parliamentary initiatives and clarifying relevant questions of law. The "Stenographic Service" records the proceedings of plenary assembly and committee sittings, and the section for "Petitions and Complaints" receives and deals with petitions from citizens who consider themselves unjustly treated by the administrative decisions of government authorities and therefore request help from parliament. The "Public Relations and Information" department is available to provide information to journalists and all interested citizens. The visitors' service which is part of this department looks after over 50,000 visitors per year who wish to inform themselves about the work of parliament at first hand in the Landtag. The "Protocol" section is in charge of organizing official functions of the Landtag and looking after delegations from home and abroad. The "Personnel, Administration and Documentation" department comprises the classic tasks of administration. It is responsible for managing the budget and finances of the Landtag, for preserving the historically valuable Landtag building and for the conduct of the sittings. It also includes the Archives, Library and Documentation sections, which supply the Landtag members with source materials for their parliamentary work.

The Bavarian Landtag, as the legislature and the supervisory instance for government and administration, has four important tasks. Firstly, it plays a substantial part in the *formation of the government:* it elects the Bavarian Chief Minister by secret ballot within one week after the constituting meeting and consents to the appointment (and dismissal) of ministers and secretaries of state.

The Bavarian Landtag is also the *legislative body* and responsible for budget law for the budget of the Free State of Bavaria. The bills are introduced when they are delivered to the Landtag President either by the Chief Minister in the name of the Bavarian government, from within the Landtag by individual members of parliamentary parties, by the Senate or by the people by way of a referendum. They are then dealt with in two readings in the Landtag plenum, unless the Council of Elders, a parliamentary party or 20 members move for a third reading. In the first reading, only the basic principles of a bill are discussed. If the bill is not rejected in this sitting, it is passed to the appropriate committees for further consultation. The committees discuss the bill and pass a resolution for a recommendation to the plenary assembly. In the second reading, the bill is first reported and then a general discussion takes place. Voting on the acceptance or rejection of the bill is carried out by a show of hands/by standing up, by a division or by name. The bills passed by the Landtag are then referred to the Senate. If the Senate raises well-founded objections within one month, the Landtag must decide whether these objections should be taken into account. Laws which are passed in this way in accordance with the constitution are conveyed to the Chief Minister for his signature and are then published within a week thereafter in the Bavarian Law Gazette with details of the date on which they come into force. Special rules apply to the budget, since it forms the basis for the work of the government and administration.

Since 1946, a total of 1073 government bills, 1052 Landtag members' bills and 33 Senate bills have been voted on in the Bavarian Landtag; in addition there have been 20,255 petitions. In the same period of time there have been six *referendums:* on the non-denominational Christian school (1967/68), on territorial reform (1971), on broadcasting freedom (1972), on free provision of school books and equipment (1977), on the composition of the Senate (1977) and on the law on waste management (1990). Three of these achieved the necessary majority of at least ten per cent of those eligible to vote, and only two were eventually passed: the non-denominational Christian school and the

Library of the Bavarian Landtag

View of the "permanent exhibition" on the Bavarian Parliament

freedom of broadcasting. Four further referendums related to the constitution: in 1946, the Bavarian Constitution itself was passed by the people, in 1970 the ages for voting and eligibility for election were reduced, in 1973 the Landtag electoral law was amended and in 1984 protection of the environment was added to the constitution as a state aim.

An important task of the Landtag is supervision of the executive, that is, of the Land government and the administration subordinate to it. For this purpose, the Landtag and its committees can require the appearance of the Chief Minister and of every secretary of state. Each member has the right to submit *Questions* to the government by way of the Landtag, provided the government is directly or indirectly responsible, to be answered orally during Question Time in the plenary assembly, or in writing. Important public questions addressed to the government relating to important matters *(interpellations)* may be introduced only by a parliamentary party or by 20 Landtag members in writing. The same applies to the application for a *Topical Hour*, in the course of which the members of the government answer questions on one particular topic, which must be of general interest and must fall under the competence of the Land. Since the beginning of the Bavarian Landtag, 8940 oral questions, 18,641 written questions and 291 interpellations have been answered and 93 Topical Hours have been held. One instrument of supervision and one of the most distinguished rights of the people of Bavaria is the *Right of Petition*. Every citizen is entitled to address requests and complaints to parliament in writing. During the lifetime of each parliament, almost 15,00 applications of this nature are made, and about 30 per cent are dealt with in the affirmative. The number of petitions received by the Landtag is steadily increasing. This can be regarded as an expression of the people's trust in "their" parliament.

The fourth task of the Bavarian Landtag is *cooperation in other organs of state and bodies*. Thus Landtag members belong to the following institutions: the Bavarian Verfassungsgerichtshof (Supreme Constitutional Court); the Councils for Broadcasting, for Bavarian Health, for the Media and for Bavarian Historical Monuments; the Advisory Council at the Bavarian Office for Data Processing and the Advisory council attached to the Bavarian Representative for Data Protection; the Bavarian Land Foundation; and the Bavarian Sports Council.

The Bavarian Senate

The Bavarian Senate assembled on 4th December 1947 for its constituting meeting in the Great Hall of the University of Munich. From 16th February 1949 it too found its final home in the Maximilianeum.

"The senate is the representative body of the social, economic, cultural and communal corporations of the Land" (Article 34, Bavarian Constitution) and convened to participate in the legislation of the Land of Bavaria; its function is essentially an advisory one.

The members of the Senate are elected not by popular election but by the respective corporations and associations, according to democratic principles. They must have reached the age of 40. They are elected for six years; every two years, the term of one-third of the senators comes to an end.

The Bavarian Senate has 60 members and is composed as follows: of eleven representatives of agriculture and forestry, five of industry and trade, five of handicrafts, eleven of the trade unions, four of the professions, five each of the cooperatives, religious communities and charitable organizations, three of the universities and academies and six of the communes and associations of communes.

By standing orders the Senate has given itself six committees: the committee for scrutiny of votes, the committee for financial matters and the budget, the committee for law and the constitution, the committee for the economy, social policy and health, and the committee for cultural policy.

Each senator is appointed for six years; every two years, the term of one-third of the senators comes to an end.

The senators, like the Landtag representatives, have a free mandate and enjoy the rights of immunity and indemnity. No-one may by a member of the Landtag and of the Senate at the same time.

View of Munich from the Maximilianeum ▷

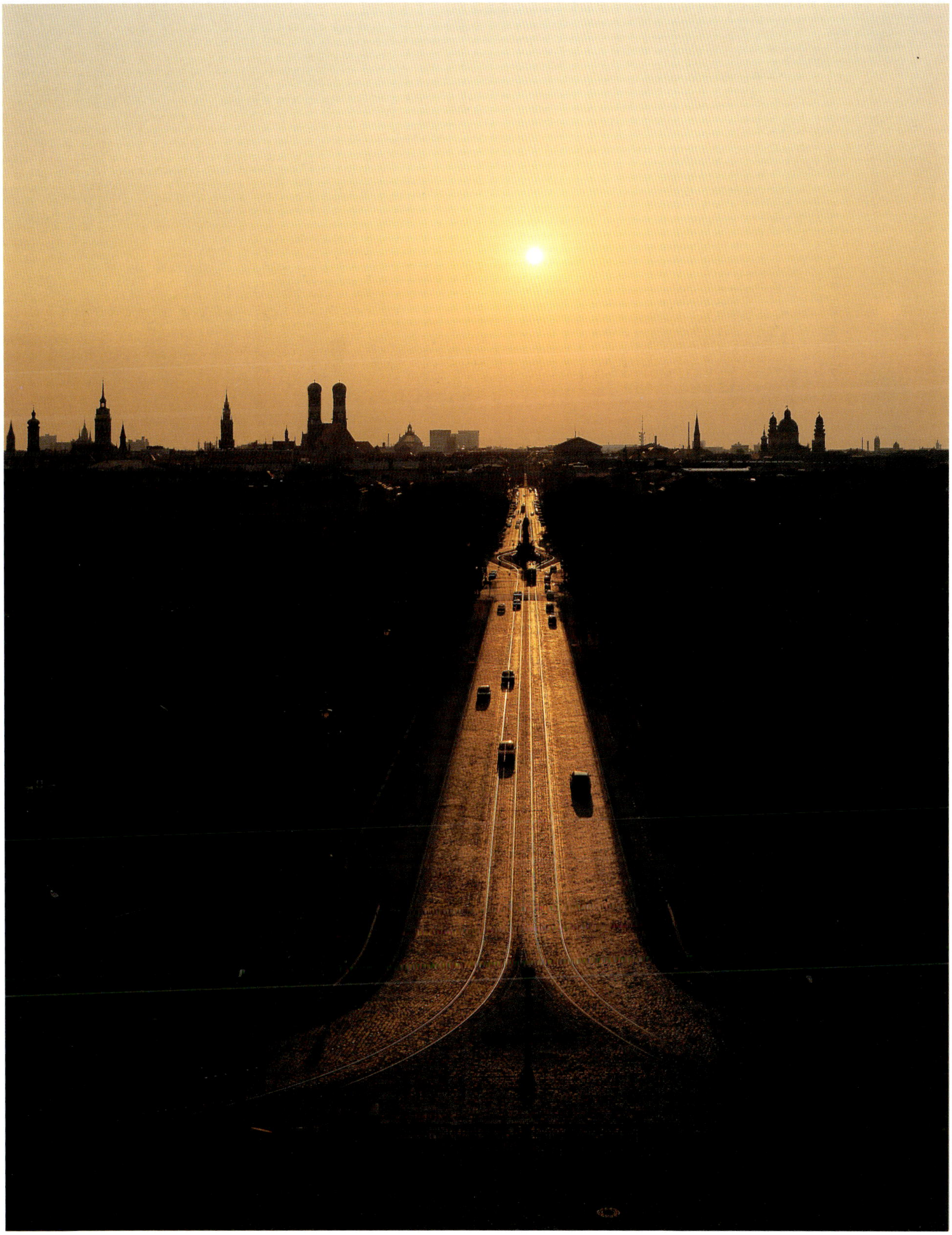

Literature

Geheimes Hausarchiv München, NL Max II. 78/3/140. – Verzeichnis der Gemälde, in: Statuten des Kgl. Maximilianeums, Munich 1884. – H. Gollwitzer (ed.), 100 Jahre Maximilianeum 1852–1952, Munich 1953. – H. Habel, Semper und der Stilwechsel am Maximilianeum, in: Jahrbuch der bayerischen Denkmalpflege 28, Munich/Berlin 1973, p. 284ff. – G. Hojer, München – Maximilianstraße und Maximiliansstil, in: Die deutsche Stadt im 19. Jahrhundert, Munich 1974, p. 33ff. – W. Nerdinger, Der Maximilianstil: Fehlgeschlagene Stilsynthese und Rückschritt der Architekturentwicklung, in: Exhibition catalogue "Gottfried von Neureuther", Munich 1978, pp. 51ff. – R.L. Bocklet (ed.), Das Regierungssystem des Freistaates Bayern, 3 vols, Munich 1977–1982. – E. Drüeke, Der Maximilianstil. Zum Stilbegriff der Architektur im 9. Jahrhundert, Mittenwald 1981. – A. Hahn, Der Maximilianstil in München. Programm und Verwirklichung, Munich 1982. – M. Dirrigl, Maximilian II., König von Bayern (1848–1864), 2 vols, Munich 1984. – R.A. Müller (ed.), König Maximilian II. von Bayern 1848–1864, Rosenheim 1988. – Die historische Entwicklung des Bayerischen Parlaments, Munich 1986. – Exhibition Catalogue "Gerd Winner: Maximilianeum", Munich 1990. – Bayerischer Landtag – Bayerischer Senat, Munich 1991 (all three publications ed. by Bayerischer Landtag, Landtagsamt). – L. Altmann, Die "Historische Gallerie" im Münchner Maximilianeum. Zur Historienmalerei unter König Max II. von Bayern, in: Weltkunst 61/18, 1991, p. 2629ff. – P.J. Kock, Der Bayerische Landtag. Eine Chronik, Munich 1991. – H. Glaser, Zur Entstehungsgeschichte der Historischen Galerie des Königs Maximilian II. von Bayern im Maximilianeum zu München, in: Musis et Litteris. Festschrift für Bernhard Rupprecht zum 65. Geburtstag, Munich 1993, p. 383ff.

Sources of Illustrations

picture archives Bavarian Landtag: illus. inside front and back covers, p. 14, 15, 34, 38, 39, 51, 134/135;
picture archives, Verlag Schnell & Steiner: illus. p. 58/59;
picture service Süddeutscher Verlag: illus. p. 133;
City archives, Munich: illus. p. 32, 33;
all other photographs: Wolf-Christian von der Mülbe, Munich/Dachau
The ground plan on p. 70 was taken with kind permission, with some alterations, from: Josef H. Biller/Hans-Peter Rasp, München Kunst & Kultur, Süddeutscher Verlag Munich 1972, p. 104

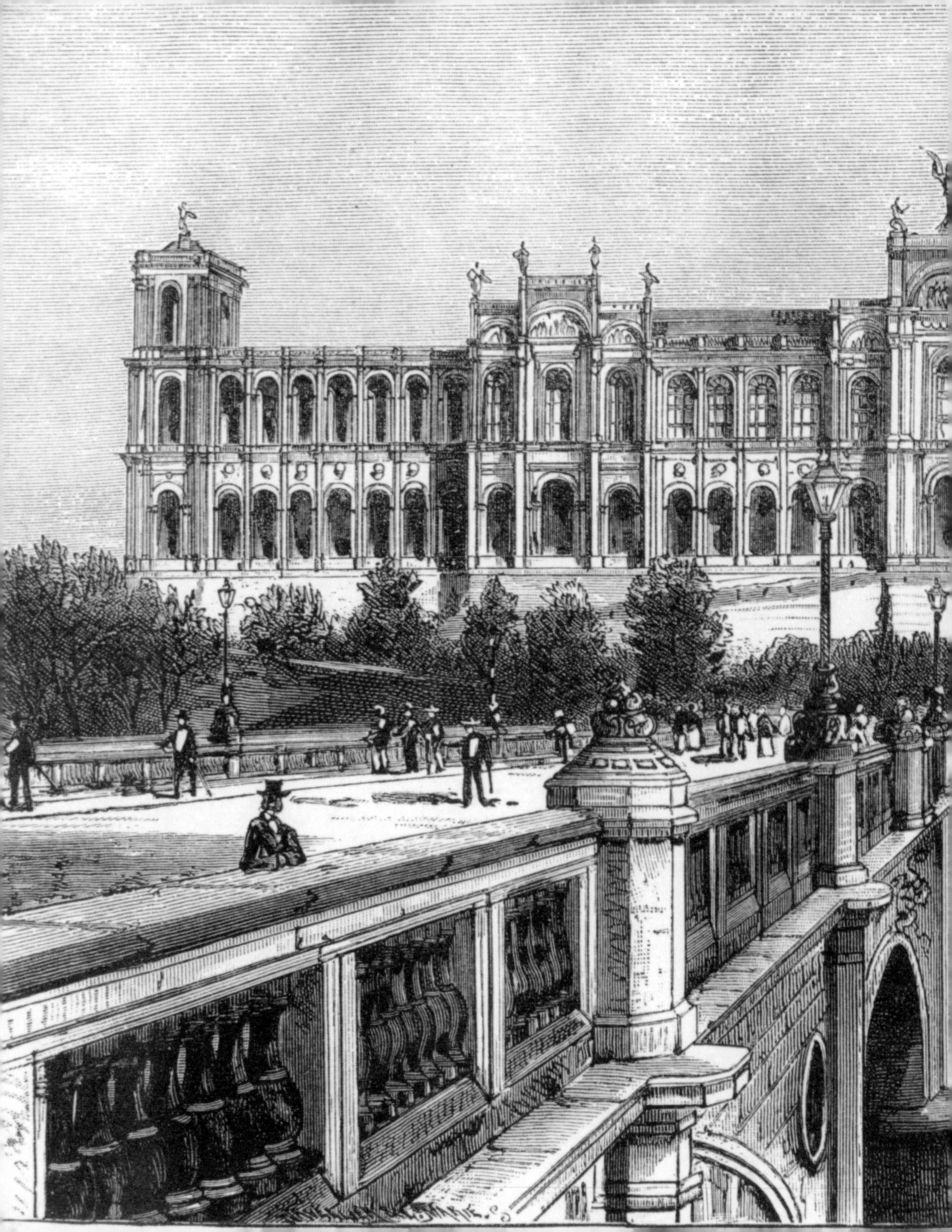